Essence of Ultimate Bliss

Meditational Self-Awareness with Twenty-one Dzogchen Nails

An Aural Transmission of
Zhang Zhung Bön Dzogchen

Essence of Ultimate Bliss

Meditational Self-Awareness
with Twenty-one Dzogchen Nails

*An Aural Transmission of
Zhang Zhung Bön Dzogchen*

**Commentary by
Geshe Dangsong Namgyal**

Root Text translation by Prof. Kurt Keutzer

Namkha Publications
Richmond, California

NAMKHA PUBLICATIONS
Richmond CA 94804 USA

COPYRIGHT ©2023 GESHE DANGSONG NAMGYAL

FIRST EDITION

ALL RIGHTS RESERVED.
No part of this book may be reproduced or transmitted in any form or by any means, electronic or mechanical, including photocopying, recording, or by any information storage and retrieval system, without permission in writing from the publisher.

ISBN: 978-0-9996898-5-1

Library of Congress Control Number: 2023916655

Contents

Foreword vii
Introduction 1
Nail. 1   Direct Revelation 8
Nail. 2   Primordially Free of Delusion 18
Nail. 3   Encompassing all without Partiality 26
Nail. 4   Unobscured Self-awareness 30
Nail. 5   Body of Bon 34
Nail. 6   Perfect Union 42
Nail. 7   Emanation Body 46
Nail. 8   Cutting Appearances 50
Nail. 9   Three Lamps 58
Nail. 10 Path without Deviation 64
Nail. 11 Lamp that Dispels Darkness 70
Nail. 12 Three Vital Points 76
Nail. 13 Pointing out the Mandala 82
Nail. 14 Single Sphere 88
Nail. 15 Manifesting is the Result 92
Nail. 16 Transcendent Equanimity 104
Nail. 17 Ultimate Dissolution 112
Nail. 18 Generating Bodhichitta 120
Nail. 19 Time of the Bardo 126
Nail. 20 Dispelling Extreme Misconceptions 138
Nail. 21 Manifesting the Result 150
Epilogue 159
How to Meditate 160
Questions and Answers 163
Acknowledgments 171
About Geshe Namgyal 172

Dedication

This book is dedicated to all my kind, wise teachers in great appreciation of their tireless guidance. It is offered especially for the benefit and liberation of all organizers, sangha and volunteers of Kunsang Gar International, in addition to the ultimate realization of all sentient beings. May all negative energies in the world be pacified.

Forward

Geshe Dangsong Namgyal is a true Rimé (ris med) lama in both his view and his studies. In his view, he is open and appreciative to the viewpoints expressed in each of Tibet's great schools: Bön, Nyingma, Sakya, Kagyu, and Gelugpa. Moreover, he has endeavored to further acquaint himself with the various views of western culture embodied in western religions and philosophy.

As for his studies, in his formal education he not only obtained a Geshe degree at the Bön Monastery Triten Norbutse, but he augmented his studies at the Gelugpa monastery Sera Je. This auxiliary study shows his genuine passion for learning, and the depth of his understanding of the Gelugpa tradition was demonstrated when the highly respected Gelugpa lama H.E. Chöden Rinpoche asked Geshe to be the resident teacher at one of his western centers. Beyond his formal studies, Geshe has taken the time to read the literature of each of the other schools of Tibet.

In my own studies with Geshe, I am always impressed by the breadth of his knowledge. From practical rituals associated with the practice of Walchen Gekhö, to his understanding of long vanished schools of madhyamaka schools' philosophy, Geshe never ceases to surprise me with the scope of his understanding. Equally importantly, he is always willing to take time to respond to questions: from minor clarifications of Tibetan terms to overall perspectives of view.

Geshe Namgyal brings all of these skills to his commentary on the *Essence of Ultimate Bliss: Meditational Awareness with Twenty-one Dzogchen Nails*. Dzogchen is the highest teaching of Bön, and *The Aural Tradition of Zhang Zhung* is universally regarded as the highest tradition of Dzogchen in Yungdrung Bön. Within the *Aural Tradition of Zhang Zhung*, the *21 Nails or Seals* belongs to the fourth and highest "utmost secret" section in which the teachings are presented to give irreversible certainty in the natural state.

While "highest teaching" is liberally applied to teachings to inspire students, the *Twenty-one Nails* is truly one of the highest teachings in all of Yungdrung Bön. It was not so long ago that students would only be introduced to these teachings after years of study and completing preliminary practices. However, given the modern situation, Geshe-la and other Bön teachers are making these teachings available to the west. Still, for many students, the pithy expressions of the 21 Seals are too abstract to be easily understood, and some complain that each seal just repeats the same points over and over. To remedy this Geshe has compassionately taken the time to give an easily accessible commentary.

— Kurt Keutzer

Essence of Ultimate Bliss

<u>Meditational Self-Awareness
with Twenty-one Dzogchen Nails</u>

*An Aural Transmission of
Zhang Zhung Bon Dzogchen*

In this teaching we often use the word *Kuntuzangpo (kun tu bzang po)* because it is the beginning of the lineage. People might think this is the name of an important Lama. If you learn the material in these chapters, you will understand the real Kuntuzangpo. This teaching has a distant and a recent lineage, and it all leads back to Kuntuzangpo; in Sanskrit, it is Samantabhadra or Dharmakaya.

In terms of lineages of the oral transmission of Zhang Zhung Dzogchen, there are four basic lineages. An emanation of Kuntuzangpo appeared in the form of Tapihritsa, who in turn, taught the instruction of oral transmission to the great master Nangzher Lopo. This is recognized as the short lineage. Nangzher Lopo was the guru of Zhangzhung's king. He met the emanation body of Kuntuzangpo three times and received all of the teachings of the oral transmission of the Dzogchen. He was the first to set the scripture down in writing which he received from Tapihritsa. Afterwards, this teaching became a dominant Bön text given by many masters throughout Zhang Zhung and Tibet.

In addition, because of the differences in practitioners and the different ways that various practitioners come to realization, there are four parts to this instruction: outer, inner, secret, and extremely secret categories.

The first outlines the tenet systems and philosophies in the general teachings in the first eight of the nine ways or vehicles of Bön. It then shows how the teaching of pure Natural Mind[1] cuts through all of those; it cuts through all the preconceived ideas that are present in the lower tenet systems. In Tibetan, it is called *tawa chig-chod (lta*

---

[1] The terms Natural Mind and Natural State both represent the Tibetan term *sem nyi* or *sems nyid*, mind itself, and are synonymous. They are capitalized because they are ultimately sacred in this context. The terms, Ultimate Nature and Ultimate Reality, are likewise used synonymously.

ba ci spyod); the 'view which cuts through all at once.'

The second category is called *manga markhrid (man ngag dmar khrid)* in Tibetan. Literally, *the Red Instructions*, it means extremely explicit instructions and is a very definitive direct transmission of instruction.

The third part deals with the naked awareness of the instruction itself—as if someone takes off their clothes and you see their body nakedly. This is called *rig pa cherthong (rig pa gcer mthong)* in Tibetan, or seeing naked awareness. This category primarily reveals the actual nature of self-knowing wisdom, *rigpa*.

The fourth part points to the Ultimate Nature of existence, the Ultimate Reality, which leads directly to the source and cuts through all doubt, leading to deep certainty about it. This is called *nelug phug chod (gnas lugs phug cod)*, or cutting through to ultimate reality.

The two types of instructions in this *Dzogchen (rdzogs chen)* teaching of the Zhang Zhung Oral Lineage are the *ka gyud (bka' rgyud)* or oral explanation lineage, and *nyam gyud (nyams rgyud)*, the experiential lineage.

The scriptural lineage is extremely vast and contains many volumes, many of which precede this teaching. However, this teaching is a part of the first category of teachings: the 'view which cuts through all at once.' The entire subject of Dzogchen practice is included within it. By practicing these instructions, it is as if you do not need any other Dzogchen instructions; it is all complete within this teaching. Both *trechöd (khreg chod)*, the cutting through, and *thögal (thod rgal)*, the direct crossing, are included. Yet it is quite short and, if you do study other teachings, this teaching can serve as a commentary to those other teachings.

I prostrate to Kuntuzangpo, the greatly compassionate one.

This all-pervasive Kuntuzangpo is not something far away or distant from us; it is within ourselves. The very nature of our mind, our own Natural State, is Kuntuzangpo. It is all-pervasive, spreading everywhere, like space, in which all the elements and phenomena are contained. Similarly, all of existence, pure and impure, samsara and nirvana, arise out of our own Natural State. That is why it is called all-pervasive. Calling it the great compassionate one is from the point of view of its quality of illuminating clarity. It contains all of the noble attributes of the Buddhas and Bodhisattvas spontaneously present within it: the six perfections, the five paths, the ten grounds and so on. Prostrating to it means that we recognize these amazing qualities and are inspired to practice that we may uncover them for ourselves.

The text states:

In order to lead the fortunate to the base stream-of-consciousness,

This essence of the profound oral transmission, highest and most secret,

This instruction that cuts to the fundamental base of the Natural State

Reveals the very pinnacle of the ultimate vehicle of the door of Bön.

Here it is saying that the instructions are for fortunate beings to investigate and discover the Natural State, the Natural Mind within themselves.

Drawn out as the essence of scripture and the heart of the tantras,

It is sacredly given as a quintessential instruction as precious as your eyes.

This oral transmission by words, and heart transmission by thought, was written in turquoise on paper as white as a conch.

This instruction has been called the door of Bön. Out of all the teachings of Buddha, it is the most precious of them all. This teaching, brought down to us by the Masters, is as precious as our eyes.

The emanation, Tapihritsa, taught it to the karmically-linked Shen,

And it was passed, in turn, to the later lineage holders.

May these nails of the twenty-one vital points

Pierce their target: the intellects of fortunate beings!

Samaya!

When it speaks of the emanation, it is referring to that aspect of Kuntuzangpo which emanated as the Lama who set this down in writing. It is presented in twenty-one sections that are called nails. The reason they are called nails is because once something is nailed down, it cannot move. It is very stable; it has no other meaning.

Nail 1

I prostrate to Kuntuzangpo, who directly reveals innate self-awareness.

A person profoundly fearing birth and death,
In a delightful solitary retreat hermitage.

The first thing a person should do is recognize the base-of-all, and gain deep certainty in innate self-awareness.

The King of innate awareness of the intrinsically born is profound and subtle. It is rarely known and hard to realize. Therefore, this distinctive method of recognition is taught.

The path of the method for discriminating between mind and the Natural Mind is:

Restrain the vital points of the body.

Hold the horse of the wind.

Let the doors of the lamp rest naturally.

As for the quintessential instruction on the discrimination between mind and the Natural Mind:

Do not scrutinize outer [objects].

Do not analyze the internal [mind].

Do not chase after the past or the future.

This teaches the full extent of the distinction between mind and Natural Mind.

When impurities dissolve into vastness, then purity radiates as light.

When the clothes of the intellect are removed, innate awareness nakedly arises.

When the clouds of thought are dispersed, primordial wisdom is freed from obscurations.

As for recognizing the mind and Natural Mind:

Free of thoughts,

Becoming the base of all,

Neutral,

Possessing the potential to arise as anything without ceasing–

These four.

The base-of-all is Natural Mind,

Recollected and aware,

Able to arise as anything whatsoever,

Liberated when released,

If allowed to settle, it mixes [with the base-of-all]—

These four.

The intellect is the mind.

As for profound certainty regarding mind and Natural Mind:

Renounce distracted actions through the three restraints.

Rest the mind in composure through the three relaxations.

Hold to the ground of innate awareness through the three methods of settling.

Cut through karmic tendencies through the three non-followings.

Continuously sustain familiarity [with innate awareness] through the three cords.

Protect the meaning from declining through the three hidings.

Exercise the dynamic energy of innate awareness through the three arisings.

Release into nonduality through the three liberations.

Uphold full measure of the result through the three non-obscurations.

This completes the nail of recognizing the base-of-all.

Samaya!

This first nail begins by discussing what kind of person can practice these teachings. A person who is a vessel for these teachings should have four characteristics. First, the person should be someone who dreads samsara and who dreads rebirth through the force of karma and delusion. In addition, that person dreads this for others as well, fearing their samsara and rebirth through the force of karma and delusion. This partakes of the Mahayana, the Great Way Teachings of Buddhism. It becomes very vast. The primary purpose of practicing this teaching is to be released from samsara, for yourself and others.

Also mentioned is that you should have a quiet place, a solitary retreat for practice.

The practitioner should recognize the Natural State of ones own mind. This is referred to as the 'basis of all,' in Tibetan, *kunzhi (kun gzhi)*, because it is the basis of the arising of samsaric existence as well as nirvanic existence. Why must we recognize this? Because, through recognition, there is a possibility of liberation; if it's not recognized, there is no possibility for liberation. Having recognized it, one needs to develop a deep, unshakeable certainty in the self-knowing wisdom that recognizes it. Having recognized and developed this deep, irreversible certainty, one will progress and reach the ultimate realization.

We can speak of innate awareness, the transcendent wisdom that is spontaneously born, as being the primordially pure nature that has always been there. It is called the king because it is the source from which all other states arise. It is profound because it is beyond the intellectual mind, beyond thought. It is called subtle because it is the ultimate state of existence. It is difficult to realize because it is beyond all the tenet systems which are particular to the lower vehicles. It is not understandable through those tenet systems. There are explanations which differentiate between the Natural Mind and various other types of minds—conceptual thoughts, perceptions and so forth.

On the one hand, this needs to be explained by the lama. But subsequently, it needs to be discovered through one's own experience, your own practice. Sit in the meditative posture, being aware of the seven points or five points as are generally explained, then let the doors of the lamp rest naturally.

Sit in meditation. Then the instruction is to refrain from scrutinizing outer objects, or analyzing the internal expressions of the mind, and not to chase after the past or future. In other words, while in meditation, do not pay attention to or investigate external objects of consciousness. Internally, do not set in motion any train of thought. In addition, do not concern oneself with past or future. Remain settled in the very present moment of awareness.

This is similar to having a glass of water with some silt in it; if you just let it sit, the silt will naturally settle to the bottom; the water will be left clear. Similarly, by remaining in a meditative state, conceptual thoughts and perceptions and all the activity of the mind will dissolve and settle down. As that occurs, the self-knowing or transcendent wisdom will become clearer and clearer.

Another example is taking off your clothes or robes. As

one undresses, the body nakedly appears. When concepts are taken away, the naked, Natural Mind arises.

Likewise, as clouds clear, the sun shines through. When the intellect and conceptual mind is allowed to dissolve, self-illuminating awareness shines through.

At that time, we recognize the basis of all, *Kunzhi,* as the self-knowing transcendent wisdom, the actual mode of existence, the Natural Mind. All other states of mind, conceptual minds or direct perceptions of the senses—are not part of the transcendent self-knowing wisdom. In this way, there is differentiation between Natural Mind and other mental states. You can call it the basis of all, *Kunzhi*; or you can call it *Rigpé Yeshé (rig pa'i ye shes),* Primordial Wisdom. It is beyond thought, beyond concept. It is the basis of all samsara and nirvana. It is neutral. It can arise without cessation. All qualities of Buddha are unceasing. Another word used in Tibetan is *sem nyi (sems nyid),* or mind itself. Ordinary mind is the mind that deals with thoughts to which a myriad of appearances can occur. It is very changeable, focusing on one object after another. These are ways of distinguishing ordinary mind. Ordinary mind is what functions to have different feelings. For example, we might feel good one day, then the weather turns for the worse and we do not feel as well. All these are aspects of ordinary mind, not the Natural Mind. One needs to practice in order to distinguish and fully differentiate between the two.

Practitioners need to give up or lessen their engagement in distracting activities; do not follow visions or thoughts or whatever appears in the mind. By giving up distracting activities of body, speech, and mind, we extend and sustain the meditation. Practice in a secret way. Keep it hidden. Do not talk about what the Lama said. Do not talk about what experiences you have. Do not talk about blessings that are received through the practice.

Various visions, sounds, rays, and lights, and feelings of happiness or sadness can arise. Realize they are manifestations of self-knowing wisdom. Whether you have happy, neutral, or unhappy feelings, or difficulties that arise in our life in society or relationships, realize that they are all things that appear in our mind. Realize that they are included within the base-of-all, Natural Mind.

Releasing duality through the three liberations means that our actions of body, speech and mind are realized to be nondual from Natural Mind. When we realize that even negative states of mind are not separate from this naked awareness, we realize the result. The ultimate nature of Natural Mind is Kuntuzangpo, the all-good. There is no increase; it does not become better. It is like when there are clouds—the light of the sun is not really effected. When negativities are seen without obscuration they do not obscure Natural Mind; that is the resultant state being realized. The base, the foundation, and the result are inseparable. This is the way *kunzhi* must be recognized: by applying these methods and being able to recognize it in your experience.

Nail 2

I prostrate to Kuntuzangpo who is primordially free of delusion.

A fortunate one who has abandoned worldly activities,

In an excellent place that is free of disturbing commotion,

Cuts through delusion by recognizing the conditions of delusion.

In sound the thinking mind is conquered.

In light the mind is transfixed.

In rays the dynamic energy is exercised.

In space there is irreversible certainty.

Hold the average beat of the pulse as a measure—

Not long, not short. Count uninterruptedly,

Counting 100 [heartbeats] as one [count],

After 180,000 [counts],

You come to mastery of familiarity with [the nature of]

appearances.

As for the rays of innate awareness and the cords of compassion

First, it is like a waterfall.

Second, it is like a stream flowing in a field.

Third, it is like a hawk searching for prey.

Fourth, it is like a turtle placed in a box.

Fifth, it is like the sky in which the four elements are exhausted.

This completes the nail of thoroughly investigating delusion.

Samaya!

In the Natural State, we go beyond all intellectual activity; all subject-object activity is dropped. It is in separating from that activity that Natural Mind is recognized. It is impossible to describe due to being beyond conceptual thought, beyond words. The only way to understand it is to experience it in meditation.

The second nail starts with prostration to Kuntuzangpo, primordially free of delusion. There are two characteristics. One is called *kadag (ka dag)* in Tibetan, meaning primordially pure. It has never had any obscuration, delusion, or stain. This primordially pure nature is within our own being. We prostrate to that Natural State within our own being.

What kind of a person is it that does this practice? In the best case scenario, it means someone who has given up worldly activities. But in any case, it means someone who takes this practice of meditation as more important than any worldly activity. It speaks of being in a place that is free of disturbing commotion, because if there is a lot of noise or disturbing occurrences in the vicinity, it can make it difficult to practice. If someone is going to meditate in such an environment, what do they do? They cut through delusion by recognizing the conditions of delusion.

If this is our Natural State, primordially pure, then how are we deluded? What causes us to develop ignorance and delusion and wander in samsara? This is what needs to be understood. The problem is in not recognizing appearances as the innate state. On the subtle level, there are appearances of sounds, lights, and rays that manifest as the energy of Natural Mind. The objects that we see in the world around us are the grosser forms of that. But by not recognizing these subtler appearances or visions of lights, rays and sounds, or the grosser appearances of the world as Natural Mind, we are deceived.

One occasion when this can be investigated is at the time of death, when the body and mind separate. When the elements are destroyed and disintegrate, this leaves the mind alone. Without dependence upon the channels, winds, and drops, the mind is left to rest in its Natural State. At that time, one can naturally reach the Natural

State and abide in it as if one was in meditation. At some point, as one is in the bardo or the intermediate state, lights, rays or sounds begin to appear. If a person does not recognize them as the manifestation of the energy of the Natural State, but grasps at them as self-existent or as coming from somewhere else, we are fooled—and that is how the deception occurs.

What first arises as deception is an ignorance called *lhen-kye marigpa (lhan skyes ma rig pa)* in Tibetan, meaning spontaneously born ignorance or unknowing. It starts in a subtle form. We grasp at visions as being self-existent and external to ourselves; it is a very subtle, innate instinctive ignorance. From there, the appeareance is further conceptualized and the ignorance becomes stronger. This is called *kuntag marigpa (kun btqgs ma rig pa)*, fully contrived ignorance. On the basis of it, we draw conclusions, create karma, and are born into samsara.

All of these subtler and grosser appearances are the energy of Natural Mind, but the subtler ones, those lights, rays and sounds, such as appear in the bardo, are the ones we work with to recognize as the manifestation of Natural Mind. That is why we practice gazing at the sky—to be able to recognize and identify the manifestations of light as the energy of the Natural State. When we close our eyes and block our nose and ears, there are visions and sounds that appear. On the basis of those kinds of appearances, visions and sounds, we begin to recognize them as manifestations of the Natural Mind. That is why the text mentions them.

The point here is to become very certain, firmly decided, that these are the manifestations or energy of the Natural Mind.

When your meditation is extended for lengthy periods of times as mentioned in the text—counting to 180,000, heartbeats for example—is when these visions can be experienced and recognized as the lights, sounds, and rays of self-knowing wisdom. At first, they ordinarily come in rapid succession, like a waterfall or like water streaming down a mountainside very quickly. Secondly, they come profusely, but at a slower speed, as if the water has reached a plateau and is slowly spreading out. Thirdly, they are like a hawk searching for prey; like a bird of prey hovering in space. The meditation does not move and remains stable, except occasionally, like the hawk going out for something to catch. Fourth, it is like a turtle placed in a basin; the mind doesn't go anywhere, it just stays in a very stable state. Finally, the fifth sign is like the sky. The elements are exhausted. It is like the sky, completely clear and pristine in which all visions have dissolved, leaving an empty sky-like appearance.

This process of investigating our Natural Mind, seeing how we develop ignorance, delusions and karma, starts with these subtle appearances—the sound, lights, and rays. We investigate at that subtle level. By extension, when it is recognized at that subtle level, we can understand that all the gross elements of our experience, the things we see, hear, smell, taste, and touch, are also the energy of the Natural Mind. This is a brief explanation of how the process of samsara is entered and how it can be reversed. The vast explanations of the *12 Links of Dependent*

Origination can be studied, but here, the very core of it is described in a brief way.

Nail 3

I prostrate to all-pervasive Kuntuzangpo, encompassing all without partiality.

The base-of-all, which dawns on everything in the great openness,

Is known as 'the space of the nature of bon.'

Having arisen as the nine characteristics of space,

Like the sky, it pervades the great vastness equally without making distinctions.

This completes the nail of the space of the nature of bon.

Samaya!

This nail is called all-pervasive and impartial. Its space encompasses all. Kuntuzangpo pervades all phenomena without any kind of partiality. It is everywhere. To that we prostrate.

Here, the text is speaking about the different characteristics of *bon nyi (bon nyid)*, the ultimate nature, which corresponds to the dharmadhatu nature of reality.

There are nine characteristics mentioned:

1. It pervades everywhere, like space.
2. It is continuous, unbroken.
3. It is infinite, endless.
4. It is undivided, indivisible.
5. There is no up and down to it.
6. It is immeasurable, fathomless.
7. It is inexhaustible.
8. It is unobstructed.
9. It is not narrow; it is vast and expansive.

The Ultimate Nature has these nine characteristics. When we are absorbed in meditation, these nine characteristics of the ultimate reality of Natural Mind shine forth. They are indivisible from us. This is how we recognize the Ultimate Nature.

Nail 4

I prostrate to Kuntuzangpo, unobscured innate self-awareness.

The base-of-all, which intrinsically arises in you,

Is known as 'the primordial wisdom of innate awareness of the mind's nature.'

Having arisen as the five characteristics of primordial wisdom,

It appears like the sun, which shines equally on all while remaining unsullied.

This completes the nail of the primordial wisdom of the mind's nature.

Samaya!

Here, the teaching focuses on the self-knowing awareness being unobscured. This is referring to the clarity quality or the illumining aspect present in Natural Mind. It is saying, I prostrate to that.

This base-of-all precedes samsara and nirvana, thus being the base of it. Self-awareness is present within it. It is said to have five characteristics of Primordial Wisdom, called the five transcendent wisdoms: Mirror-like Wisdom, Equalizing Wisdom, Discriminating Wisdom, All-Accomplishing Wisdom, and Wisdom Understanding Emptiness.

The description of the Wisdom Realizing Emptiness is similar to that in the Madhyamika or Middle Way tenet system; that wisdom understands emptiness or selflessness. Mirror-like Wisdom is the illumining factor or clarity factor, which reflects all things just like a mirror reflects all that passes in front of it. Discriminating Wisdom is the wisdom of discerning wisdom or individual knowing, and refers to all the qualities and realizations present within the enlightened state; but they are known individually and are not mixed together. Equalizing Wisdom is the characteristic of wisdom being present in both the enlightened state and the limited state of sentient beings—equally in both. All-Accomplishing Wisdom points to the characteristic of all activity being accomplished without striving, without effort, and without having to think it through. Because all these wisdoms are present in Natural Mind, it is referred to as self-knowing wisdom, *Rigpé Yeshé (rig pa'i ye shes)*.

33

Nail 5

I prostrate to Kuntuzangpo, primordially pure innate self-awareness.

As for the clear, self-originating king of innate awareness,

Self-originated primordial wisdom abides
as the foundation of the base-of-all.

Formless, it is primordial wisdom
beyond form, shape and color.

Inexpressible, it is primordial wisdom
beyond letters, words, and names.

Non-conceptual, it is primordial wisdom
beyond the concepts and discernment of intellect.

The primordial wisdom tsön gang (tshon gang)
is the body of bon without appearances.

Shenlha Karpo, the base-of-all beyond any designation,

Is known as "the innate awareness of the essential nature."

From the tshon gang that is the great primordial wisdom of

clarity,

Arises the tshon gang that is the great light of appearance—

Neither collected, nor separated, light arising in itself,

Clear without substance, apparent though devoid of self-nature.

Not conditioned by shape or color,

Transcending any measurement as large or small,

It is known as the 'great appearance, the body of bon.'

Shenlha Karpo, designated as the root Deity,

Is known as 'innate awareness of the appearance of special insight.

*When the eye of primordial wisdom arises
in the body of tsön gang,*

It sees all ten directions without front or back—

An unobstructed eye that sees all without looking.

Appearing as great transparency without inner or outer,

Remaining as the great pervasion, without middle or perimeter,

It is an undefiled base of all that arises.

The primordially abiding king of innate awareness

Is without elements, phases, places, nirvana, or samsara.

It arises from the beginning as the king of innate awareness.

It is not produced by Buddhas.

It does not arise from teachings.

It is not accomplished by sentient beings or by their actions.

It is not accomplished by people or by their efforts.

Because it is without cause and condition, it is naturally unproduced.

Unlike the material world, it is not made from atoms.

It is not made into a body through the action of the elements.

It is not born from a womb or produced by a father.

It is beyond samsara, it transcends the causes of delusion and of realization.

Self-originated, primordial wisdom abides as the foundation, the base-of-all.

Primordially self-arising, clear, and luminous,

[The tsön gang] is neither fabricated or destroyed, decreased or increased,

harmed or benefited, killed or revived.

Without the opposing pairs of comfort and misery, youth and aging, birth and death,

It is known as 'arising as light,' without beginning or end.

This completes the nail of the tshon gang, the body of bon.

Samaya!

This nail deals with how to think about primordial purity. Here, Natural Mind is referred to as *Rangjung Yeshe*, self-arising, self-originating primordial wisdom. It is the foundation and root of all samsara and nirvana. It's not something that has shape or form. It has no color. And it can't be engaged by anything; words, letters, terms cannot be used on it. It is beyond concept. It is beyond any kind of gross or subtle analysis or checking. Then how do we use words to describe it? We say it is transcendent wisdom that is tsön gang "thumb-sized."

This terminology is used for someone who feels they need to analyze and investigate. Saying that it is just thumb-sized conveys to the practitioner that it doesn't change. It remains the same, just as it is; it doesn't get bigger and it doesn't get smaller. This can be helpful for someone who feels they need to investigate it with words. The primordial, thumb-sized wisdom is the body of bon, *bon ku (bon sku),* without appearances. This is all referring to Dharmakaya. Another name that's given to it is Shenlha Karpo, the White Shen Deity. This tends to be a concept that people develop faith or belief in. You can also think of it that way if you wish. Karpo means white, which connotes its pure nature. It signifies its being completely free of obscuration, completely clear. It is Natural Mind, the essential nature and basis of all, the kunzhi, the foundation from which everything appears. Shenlha Karpo, the White Shen Deity, Dharmakaya, is the basis, like a root Deity from which all Deity forms and mandalas manifest without effort, spontaneously. It is not a Deity that would have a position, like a front-generated or self-generated Deity; it is a Deity that pervades all directions of space.

What kind of vision or eyes does this Deity have? Unobstructed vision everywhere. It is not like our eyes, which are obstructed; we can't see through walls. In Shenlha Karpo, everything can be seen, even with the eyes closed.

Does it have a beginning or end? No. It is beginningless and endless. It has a nature of luminosity. This is why we need to meditate. By going beyond concepts and mental activity, the light of the Natural Mind continues to shine forth. This nail conveys how to consider the Natural Mind:

without end, without beginning, the nature of light. In the context of three kayas, Dharmakaya, Sambhogakaya and Nirmanakaya, this nail pertains to how to recognize Dharmakaya.

Nail 6

I prostrate to Kuntuzangpo, the body of perfection, innate self-awareness.

From the vast expanse of the base-of-all—selfless, clear, and empty—

Arises the naturally clear, non-conceptual, primordial wisdom tsön gang.

In the non-dual equality of space and primordial wisdom,

Three appearances arise as natural, dynamic energy.

Objects and innate awareness are neither mixed nor separate.

All the myriad appearances, sounds, and thoughts are perfect.

The union of space and primordial wisdom is the treasure of great perfection.

The union of sky and expanse [of the three appearances] is the treasure of great perfection.

The union of method and wisdom is the treasure of great perfection.

The union of subject and object is the treasure of great perfection.

The union of cause and result is the treasure of great perfection.

The union of body and mind is the treasure of great perfection.

The union of vessel and essence is the treasure of great perfection.

The union of father and mother is the treasure of great perfection.

The union of body and primordial wisdom is the treasure of great perfection.

The union of deity and celestial palace is the treasure of great perfection.

This completes the nail of the body of perfect union.

Samaya!

Here we prostrate to Kuntuzangpo as self-knowing. We recognize Kuntuzangpo as present in Natural Mind.

With the words, 'From the vast expanse', a metaphor is implied: Dharmakaya, the *Bon Ku*, is like clear space, and Kuntuzangpo is like the sun within that space. Considering the two aspects, clarity and emptiness —in Kuntuzangpo they are a unity. *Yeshé (ye shes)*, primordial wisdom, is in union with *ying (dbying)*, the sphere of space. Other terms are used as well. Kuntuzangpo is described in terms of the unification of these pairs: transcendent wisdom and emptiness, internal and external space, clarity and emptiness, means and wisdom, cause and effect. With the terms means and wisdom, wisdom refers to emptiness, the side of primordial purity; means or methods refers to the clear, illuminating awareness. Because clarity is unobstructed, all the deities and mandalas can appear and are spontaneously accomplished within it. Once you have experience in meditation and have realized this, there is a unification of body and mind. That is the realization of Kuntuzangpo. Kuntuzangpo appears as the energy or manifestation of Dharmakaya, the innate Natural Mind.

Nail 7

I prostrate to Kuntuzangpo, the emanation body that is innate self-awareness.

The domain of appearances and primordial wisdom of innate awareness

are neither separated nor mixed.

They are a unified, dynamic energy,

and arise as all the myriad sights, sounds and thoughts.

The six consciousnesses and the six sense organs that are connected to the six objects

Emanate without partiality the diversity within samsara and nirvana.

They arise effortlessly as the self-originating dynamic energy.

In the space of appearances, nothing is dissolved or diminished.

The sky of innate awareness is neither clear nor obscured.

Self-originated and self-liberated, [all appearances] are complete in the single sphere.

This completes the nail of the impartial emanation body.

Samaya!

This next nail goes on to the emanation bodies, Nirmanakaya. The Ultimate Nature, Natural Mind, is Nirmanakaya as well. Once the meditator practices and develops realization, all their activities of body, speech and mind are recognized as emanation bodies, as their own Nirmanakaya. This is because, in their realization, all of these activities derive from and arise out of Natural Mind. It is difficult for a beginner to recognize, but for someone who has experienced the realization, it is understood how these activities of body, speech, and mind are the same nature, not separate from, Natural Mind. From the side of their Ultimate Nature, for the practitioner who has realized Natural Mind, all activities of body, speech and mind are realized to be Nirmanakayas. That is a brief explanation.

Nail 8

I prostrate to Kuntuzangpo, dispeller of the darkness of doubt.

The examples that illustrate the union of objects and innate awareness are

Water, crystal, the sun, and a butter lamp.

The four times of abiding, connecting, separating, and delusion

Are associated with the unobscured, clarity, and the manner of becoming obscured.

Seeing things as they are, your Buddhahood is freed.

Obtaining power over appearances, you have the mastery of a world conqueror.

Seeing self as other, sentient beings are deluded.

Chasing after appearances, they are deceived by these illusory external forces.

[Buddhas and sentient beings] emerge from the power of our nature,

Without the causes and conditions of karma.

They emerge without beginning or end, unlimited by time.

If you gain certainty in the undeluded essence, then delusion is impossible.

If you cut appearances at the source, then appearances will no longer deceive.

This completes the nail of symbolic examples.

Samaya!

The eighth nail uses exemplifying metaphors to dispel doubts. In general, Natural Mind is unobscured, not covered by anything. But the elements of our body tend to obscure it from us. At the time of death, when the elements of the body drop away, Natural Mind can clearly dawn. If, at that point, we are unable to recognize the lights, rays and sounds as the energy of our Natural Mind, the process of that awareness becoming obscured will begin again.

For the experienced, realized practitioner, any appearance or object that arises in awareness can be realized to be one nature with Natural Mind, like the sun and its rays. The reason it is called self-knowing awareness, *Rang-rig Yeshe (rang rig ye shes)*, is because any appearances or visions that arise are understood to be intrinsic to the awareness from which they have arisen. Feelings, experiences of happiness and sadness, experiences of the various objects of the senses, sights, scents, sounds, tastes, tangible objects, arising of thoughts—when all these are recognized as Natural Mind they are released or liberated.

In the context of Dzogchen, they are enlightened.

Seeing things as they are, your Buddhahood is freed. Obtaining power over appearances, you have the mastery of a world conqueror.

The same goes for ignorance and samsara. If they are seen as they are, they are liberated. You gain freedom of what appears to you. You can have control of what appearances arise. If we are skillful in our practice, this can happen without taking a very long time in this human state. With control of appearances, none of the things of samsara can harm us.

The subtle visions we are talking about are those lights, rays, and sounds that arise out of the Natural Mind. Grosser kinds of appearances include feelings of happiness and sadness, perceptions of sights, sounds, scents, and so on. Those are manifestations of the energy of the Natural Mind, but we are deceived when we are unable to recognize them or when they're seen as different and separate from ourself. By following after them or objectifying appearances, we become fooled by the illusion.

About karmic causality, at the point when the subtle appearances are not recognized as the energy of the Natural Mind, karma begins to be created again; this follows naturally. Exactly when one is deceived in regard to appearances is difficult to say. How it happens is what is being described here; how we are deceived by not being able to recognize those appearances for what they are. If we recognize the sights, sounds and rays as the energy or the manifestation of the innate Natural Mind, then it is impossible for us to be deceived by them. It is like stopping a stream at its source; there can be no water flowing from there. If, at the source of the visions arisal, you can recognize them as manifestations of the Natural Mind, the whole continuum of delusion and deception is cut and cannot flow from there. Thus, it is those appearances that deceive us.

The metaphor is that of the sun and its rays. The sun is like Natural Mind itself. The rays are like the manifestations or appearances that arise from it. Just as the sun's rays don't come from anywhere but the sun, appearances are understood to emerge from Natural Mind itself. Yet in our experiences of feelings and the objects around us, we perceive them to be existent in and of themselves. This kind of 'true self-existence' is what is refuted in the Middle Way or Madhyamika teachings. In these, we apply the reasoning of interdependence through dependent origination to prove that things don't arise just from themselves, without depending on their parts or relativity. But it is through mistaking things, such as the subtle appearances of the lights, rays, and sounds, as existing in and of themselves, that gives rise to all the kinds of sufferings we experience—in relationships, loss and so on. They appear to be things that exist outside ourselves or that affect us from an outside source. Everyone has a tendency to objectify things this way, even though they are not established as truly separate, external things.

There is deep meaning in the assertion of some of the tenet systems that everything is created by mind, or everything is mind. Here, in these Dzogchen teachings, it is even more profound: that everything is the nature of that ultimate reality of Natural Mind. The point of practice in the course of our lives, when we meet with different experiences of suffering and so on, is to see them like this example of the sun and its rays, or like the clarity of a crystal and the appearances reflected in it.

Nail 9

I prostrate to Kuntuzangpo, who neither meets with nor departs from innate self-awareness.

The primordial wisdom of innate self-awareness is hidden and concealed.

The heart that is the abiding-ground

Is like the ocean or the expanse of sky.

The heart of the light of appearances

Is like a pavilion of five-colored rainbow light.

The limited heart of flesh

Is like an alloyed, jeweled vase.

The clear primordial wisdom tsön gang

Is like a lamp inside that vase.

These three—sound, light, and rays—

Are like the dynamic energy of the rays from a lamp.

The king, innate awareness, arises from within.

The base-of-all arises from the vastness of emptiness.

Appearances arise from the [inner] chamber of light.

Illusion arises from the center of the body.

The treasure of the sky, the perfect source-of-all,

Becomes obscured through the successive layering of stains.

If there is no portal, it will not be seen.

Opening the door to the treasure reveals the source of the treasure.

This completes the nail of innate self-awareness that emerges from within.

Samaya!

This nail discusses Kuntuzangpo, Natural Mind, as being something that we never meet or part from. It is always here. There is no meaning added to it. As soon as we are living beings, that innate self-awareness is here; we're never separated from it. This primordial wisdom is something that exists within us in a hidden manner. Obscured by the elements of the body, awareness wisdom is hidden. However, the quality of it can emerge through the practitioner's own subtle level body's channels, energies and drops being activated. Awareness has many supporting factors that appear from the subtle body's phenomenon. When we are practicing and we ask *'where does this ultimate nature abide?,'* we can say that it resides in our heart. Through the channel from the heart to the eyes, it is said that this ultimate nature can be seen through the *'door of the eyes,'* such as when the lights and rays appear. We say that we see open nature, or we see signs of it. Because of this, when practitioners meditate in dark rooms where all the light has been completely blocked out, they are able to read letters and words. This is a result of the clear light of the Natural Mind appearing.

That light is not seen through the physical organ of the eye or eye consciousness. It is seen by the luminosity itself, coming out of the Natural Mind. It is like a lamp that has been placed inside a vessel—it is hidden inside the elements of the body. It is because of that light of the ultimate nature, the qualities of Natural Mind shining forth, that practitioners are able to see in the dark. When practicing direct crossing *(thögal)* and looking at the light of the sky or sun, when various colors or shapes are seen, it is different qualities of Natural Mind appearing. Obscured by the body, appearances arise from the Natural State through the door of the eyes. There are other reasons these appearances are obscured; for example, due to our strong grasping at objects and because of karmic traces arising.

In general, there are said to be three lamps by which the Natural Mind is revealed. The first lamp is through explanations and instructions being given. The second is by perceiving qualities of the Natural Mind arising through the lamp of the eyes. The third is the lamp of realizing Natural Mind itself. We need to seek out these avenues of discovering this great treasure within us— by way of hearing the teachings, by way of the thögal practice of looking at the sky and seeing visions, and by manifesting Natural Mind through meditation. This is the nail of self-awareness arising from within. Like a lamp obscured within a vessel, by using the methods of hearing instructions, seeing signs, and manifesting self-awareness, Natural Mind is allowed to shine forth from within.

Nail 10

I prostrate to Kuntuzangpo, innate self-awareness that is straight and whole.

From the primordial wisdom tsön gang, innate self-awareness,

Emerge the five reflected lights of appearances.

From those arise the five pure ones.

From those arise the five gross ones.

Through these twenty-five, body and mind are produced.

Innate awareness arises through the path of the channel.

Emanating above, it is the path of nirvana.

Emanating below, it is the path of samsara.

Moving in the right [channel], it is the path of defects.

Moving in the left [channel], it is the path of positive qualities.

The three doors are the path to samsara of the three realms.

Arising in the four doors is the path of four types of birth.

Arising in the five doors is the path of five migrations.

Arising in the nine orifices is the path of nine places.

*The central channel is the path of nonduality
of samsara and nirvana.*

The king of innate awareness arises from that path.

[It] arises from the space of emptiness, the base-of-all.

[It] arises from the [inner] chamber of light.

[It] arises from the bodhicitta mind stream, the central channel.

Undefiled innate awareness is the path of authenticity.

Great primordial wisdom is the path of clarity.

That which is straight and whole is the path of the sphere.

This is not a door to the path of samsara.

The rider—the mind of innate awareness—

Is mounted on the horse of mindfulness.

Unimpededly propelled by wings of the wind,

It moves through the path of the bodhicitta central-channel

And arrives at the secret door of bliss at the crown.

The king of innate awareness nakedly arises.

Concepts—the clothes of the intellect—are removed.

Self-originated primordial wisdom sees its own face.

Ignorance—the darkness of delusion—is lifted.

The three realms and nine grounds are shaken from their depths.

The continuity of the path of five mental-afflictions is broken.

The ocean of six types [of migration] in samsara is dried up.

The four types of birth—the portals of samsara—are emptied.

The seal of the self-arising three bodies is opened.

This completes the nail of the path without deviation.

Samaya!

From primordial wisdom, that thumb-sized innate self-awareness, from this Dharmakaya, described as without thought and not changing, arises five different colors of light. How do these lights arise and how does samsara and nirvana arise from them? In one simple way, when someone asks how the world is created, this is how. From this Natural Mind arise the five clear ones, *dang ma (dang's ma)*, and then the five elements. *Dang ma*, clear ones, means elements, but in their subtle forms, their essence. Not like the external elements we see, like fire and water—those are more like residue of the subtler forms of the elements. The elements we make use of, with solidity, moisture, heat, and so on, are what is left over from the subtler forms of the elements. It is out of the grosser elements that our bodies are formed. Material substance of the elements, heat from fire, cohesiveness and moistness of water, movement of air, solidity of earth—these are what form our body.

Through the psychic channels of the body, the subtle path of the channels, the Natural Mind can appear.

There is said to be two types of channels: channels in which delusions flow through our body and channels of transcendent wisdom. In some texts these are related to the left and right channels that run next to the central channel. In that context the right channel is said to be the deluded channel and the left channel is said to be the one in which primordial wisdom flows. It's the way that the energy flows in these channels that effect the practitioner in recognizing the Natural State. Whether they practice or not makes a difference in how they will take rebirth. If those energies can be influenced and brought into the central channel, it is very conducive for taking higher rebirth. It can be a higher state within samsara. Beyond that, if it's recognition of the Natural Mind itself, it can also mean attainment of liberation or enlightenment. In connection with transference of consciousness or phowa, when awareness is ejected through the central channel of the body, it can lead to fortunate rebirth. And if that practice is conjoined with recognition of Natural Mind, the ultimate nature of the mind, it leads to liberation and enlightenment as well. At that point it is no longer obscured by the body or by conceptual thought, so the self-knowing Natural Mind can nakedly appear.

Our meditation practice is intended for this purpose—to remove obscurations and let the innate state shine forth. We work towards this. We want to remember that this is what we are doing, so that at the time of death we know what we are doing.

The seal is opened so that the three bodies can shine forth. It is said that when we obtain control or freedom of the three bodies, we come to understand that they are our own. When you know you have something you can use it.

Nail 11

I prostrate to Kuntuzangpo, dispeller of the darkness of ignorance.

The primordial wisdom of innate self-awareness arises in the five doors.

The five objects appear clearly and without thoughts.

It is the intellect that conceives objects.

The path of seeing innate awareness is the door of the lamp.

Through the watery lamp of the far-reaching lasso,

The darkness of the world is dispelled.

Through the lamp of appearances of special insight,

The darkness of intellect's tendency toward nihilism is dispelled.

Through the lamp of primordial wisdom of innate self-awareness,

Ignorance, darkness of the intellect, is dispelled.

Through the lamp of space of the base-of-all,

Darkness of the judgmental intellect is dispelled.

The king of innate awareness arises in seeing.

The base-of-all arises in the empty sky.

Appearances arise in the inner sphere of light.

The clarity-of-all arises in the door of the lamp.

Like a lotus emerges from the mud,

The king of innate awareness emerges from the [inner] chamber.

Just as the sun is separate from darkness,

The king, innate awareness, is separated from dark obscuration.

The six eyes of special insight arise at the forehead.

Naked seeing is perfect knowledge.

This completes the nail of the lamp that dispels darkness.

Samaya!

It is the characteristic of Kuntuzangpo or Samantabadra-Dharmakaya that is being brought up here. The ignorance that has kept us bound in the samsaric situation is very deep and dark. The Dharmakaya lamp of the Natural Mind is so powerful, however, that it is like bringing a light into a room; even though it was completely dark before, it is instantly illuminated. Recognizing that the slightest awareness of Natural Mind can eliminate eons of ignorance and darkness, we prostrate to that quality of Dharmakaya Natural Mind.

It is being compared to a lamp that illuminates awareness of Natural Mind, as well as eyes that can perceive signs of the Natural State. They are both referred to as lamps. Natural Mind has this facet of emptiness. It is sometimes referred to as *ying*, the sphere of space. Why is it called a lamp? A mind that grasps at things sees only a part of them. It is partial—and that is associated with ignorance. Whereas, the ultimate nature of Natural Mind pervades everything. It is not partial. It is a lamp that dispels darkness of grasping and partiality.

When we use methods to manifest Natural Mind, it happens like a flower that rises out of the mud. Like that, Natural Mind can appear out of the elements of the body. Like sunlight breaking through the clouds, Natural Mind can shine through obscurations of the body. This is primarily referring to thögal practice, direct crossing. In thögal practice there are different postures of the body that can be used for meditation that enable the Natural State to shine forth. Special signs can appear, different from the usual signs of meditation. Sometimes the practitioner will see drops of light or many drops of light, and those can remain for long periods of time. Superior seeing is referred to as *lhagthong (lhag mthong)* in Tibetan, or *vipassana* in Sanskrit, but different from the vipassana of sutra teachings.

Some Dzogchen teachings say that these kinds of special signs do not appear during the first stage of trechöd; they only appear in the more advanced thögal, direct crossing practice. In that context we call thögal *lhak tong*, seeing beyond. These kinds of special visions must come through manifesting Natural Mind; otherwise, just seeing them with your eyes is not that significant. It is said that through the trechöd practice, the cutting through practice, the entire results of Dzogchen can be realized. But if, through trechöd, you can't yet come to the realization of empty forms or clear light, then thögal can bring that about. It is in the trechöd practice that certainty is developed; with trechöd practice alone, the entire resultant state can be realized. The thögal practice of looking at the lights is for realizing that the visions that appear are the energy of Natural Mind arising. My personal opinion is that trechöd and thögal were not two separate categories in Ancient Bon Dzogchen, but that this idea developed as popular Nyingma Dzogchen and Bon Dzogchen influenced each other. This could be a subject for further research.

Nail 12

I prostrate to Kuntuzangpo, the inseparable union of the three bodies.

The primordially pure wisdom of innate self-awareness is the body of bon.

The connection between body and mind is the complete enjoyment body.

The performer of various deeds is the emanation body.

Because the base innate awareness arises from within, it is an inseparable union with essence.

Because it is trained in the channel, the path of innate awareness, it is a path without deviation.

Because the result arises in the door, the three bodies are not covered by obscurations.

Innate self-awareness, the body of bon, is in the vastness of the heart.

The natural complete body is in the path of the channel.

The self-arising emanation body is in the door of the lamp.

From within, self-arising abides as the primordially enlightened state.

From the inner-sphere, spontaneous perfection emerges as the completely enlightened state.

In the act of seeing, the unobscured is seen as the manifestly enlightened state.

Through recognizing the base-of-all, the mother, the Natural State, is met.

Through drawing out primordial wisdom from its hiding place, the darkness of obscurations is dispelled.

Through pulling out the naked innate awareness, the three bodies are manifested.

When the conditions of delusion are recognized, the root of delusion is cut.

When the Natural State is pointed out, all doubts of the dualistic mind are dissolved.

When the door of the treasury of innate awareness is opened,

You break through to the innermost treasury of the base-of-all.

This completes the nail of pointing out the three vital points.

Samaya!

In this twelfth nail, we prostrate to Kuntuzangpo as the inseparable union of the three kayas of Buddha. This ultimate nature is present in every being, whether they realize it or not. This nail is teaching about how to recognize and see the three kayas as present in Natural Mind. The three bodies are always present in ourselves and are inseparable. Primordially pure wisdom, innate self-awareness, the bon body, dharmakaya, has been forever present. The connection between body and mind is the Sambhogakaya, the complete enjoyment body. The activities of body, speech and mind, which are never separate from innate self-awareness, are the emanation bodies, the Nirmanakayas. Whenever we act with body, speech or mind, they are never newly met or never separated from, but emanating from Natural Mind. In thögal practice the innate state can shine forth through the path of the psychic channels. Through perceiving these signs of the innate Natural State or Natural Mind, we can be unmistaken about the nature of our actions of body, speech and mind. The three kayas of Buddha are always unobscured in the Natural State, never leaving it, never going outside Natural Mind. The Dharmakaya, the bon body, the *bonku*, must be recognized at the heart center. The movement of the energies in the channels of the body is the Sambhogakaya. The energies that flow within the channels is the Samboghakaya. The signs that are seen through the lamp of the eyes are the Nirmanakaya. That appearance from within the heart of Natural Mind is the Primordial Buddha, Dharmakaya.

In the act of seeing, the unobscured is seen as the manifestly enlightened state. The signs that are seen through the eyes and heard through the ears are the Nirmanakaya, the innate Natural State residing, hidden at the heart, brought out and seen through the eyes.

When conditions of delusion are recognized, the root of delusion is cut. When the visions of light, rays and sound appear and are not recognized as the energy of the innate state, we are deceived by grasping them as truly existent. But when we can cut through that and see that they are in fact emanations or energy of Natural Mind, we can cut through the very root and ultimate source of delusions.

When the Natural State is pointed out, all doubts of the dualistic mind are dissolved. When there is a very direct pointing out of the ultimate, Natural State of the mind, just as if you were pointing to an object with your finger, then the undecided mind of doubt is exhausted.

When the door of the treasury of innate awareness is opened, you break through to the innermost treasury of the base-of-all. Through doing the practice, the door opens to a great treasure of awareness within us—Natural Mind. It is the very root of all, the *kunzhi*, the foundation of samsara and nirvana. The words of the text are poetic but what is most important is to connect directly with the meaning.

Nail 13

I prostrate to Kuntuzangpo, the root deity of innate self-awareness.

As for revealing the spontaneously perfected mandala of symbolic forms,

The clear and empty vast expanse of the base-of-all is the space of the nature of bon.

The primordial wisdom, tshon gang, is the self-arising body of bon.

Sound, light, and rays are the complete enjoyment body.

The three miraculous emanations are the bodies of various emanations.

The five lights of appearance are the base of the mandalas of the pure realms.

The pavilion of the sphere is the celestial palace of the five Buddha families.

The body of special insight emerges as various form bodies.

The three miraculous emanations are the bodies of various emanations.

The five lights of appearance are the base of the mandalas of the pure realms.

The pavilion of the sphere is the celestial palace of the five Buddha families.

The body of special insight emerges as various form bodies.

The three unions are the base of the emanation of the three bodies.

The five deities, the five bodies, the five [Buddha] families, the five primordial wisdoms,

The principal couple, and their retinue are emanations that cannot be comprehended by thought.

The great mandala is naturally accomplished without effort.

The mandala of three bodies is completed in bodhicitta.

Because the mandala arises within oneself, there is neither effort nor accomplishment.

Because appearances lack any inherent nature, there is neither desire nor attachment.

This completes the nail of pointing out the mandala.

Samaya!

In this thirteenth nail, we prostrate to Kuntuzangpo, the root deity of innate self-awareness. In the Dzogchen tradition, Kuntuzangpo is the root deity of innate self-awareness, *Rangrig Yeshe*. With two facets, it is primordially pure, empty, and spontaneously accomplished. All the qualities and realizations of Buddha are present within it. They can arise at any time, without obstruction. This facet of Kuntuzangpo being the root deity refers to this spontaneous quality.

All the various Buddha aspects—the five Buddha families, the peaceful and wrathful Yidam meditational deities, the protectors and so on—they all arise out of this root deity, the ultimate nature of mind. That self-aware, transcendent wisdom is the root deity, the root of all the Buddha and deity forms. Therefore, when you practice this awareness of Natural Mind, all of the Buddhas and meditational deities are included in it. Here we prostrate to Kuntuzangpo with the understanding that it is the root of all Buddha forms.

There are two aspects to transcendent wisdom: self-arising and self-knowing. In general, the empty, ultimate nature of the Natural State is characterized as Dharmakaya. Its empty aspect is called *Rangjung Yeshe*, the self-arising transcendent wisdom. The thumb-sized Dharmakaya can also be recognized as this self-arising wisdom. The self-knowing aspect of it is called *Rangrik Yeshe*, self-knowing transcendent wisdom. Thus, self-arising is the empty aspect and self-knowing is the aware aspect. The manifestations that appear within this unified, self-aware, self-arising transcendent wisdom are the pure lands and mandalas of Buddhas. These include the five pure lands of the five families of Buddhas in their male/female unified form, *Yab-Yum* in Tibetan, as well as the principals and entourages of all the mandalas. In the general procedure of tantric teachings, each deity is to be realized and actualized separately. These kinds of practices involve a lot of conceptual thought and effort which, in this case, is seen as a lot of grasping. That is not the mode of presentation here. Rather, out of Natural Mind, all these things arise very naturally and effortlessly, like waves emerging out of the ocean. Like reflections of the moon in water, when the ultimate Natural State is realized, the Buddhas, deities, and mandalas appear effortlessly. But when such Buddha forms, mandalas, pure lands arise out of the Natural State, if one gets involved with conceptual dualistic kinds of thinking, for example, thinking 'how great!'—then they are lost! That leaves nothing else to do but practice. Instead, view them as being the very nature or manifestation of Natural Mind, never joining with it or separating from it. That's the main point that is being presented in this thirteenth nail.

Nail 14

I prostrate to Kuntuzangpo, the self-originated single body.

The nature of mind is the essence of mind.

The sky is the natural radiance of mind.

The nature of bon is the ultimate mind—pervasive, without inner and outer.

All appearances are the play of body.

All sounds are the play of speech.

All thoughts are the play of mind.

All events are the play of positive qualities.

All that is done is the play of enlightened activity.

All is completed within the single sphere.

This completes the nail of pointing out the single [sphere].

Samaya!

In this fourteenth nail, prostration is made to Kuntuzangpo within a body, a self-arisen single sphere. Self-arisen means that it does not take any effort to create this self-arising, single sphere. Within the single self-arisen wisdom, both skillful means and wisdom are present; they don't need to be practiced separately. This term for single sphere, *nyag chig (nyag gcig)* in Tibetan, means that it cannot be divided up by thought.

Natural State is the essence of the mind. Space is the natural radiance of the mind. This refers to a natural characteristic of the mind being infinite, without edges, without end. The ultimate state is the ultimate nature, referred to as the *bon nyi*, the Bön nature. This is the ultimate nature of Natural Mind. It pervades all outer and inner things: all the aggregates and elements of the body within and external appearances without.

All appearances are the play of body. All sounds are the play of speech. All thoughts are the play of mind. For someone who is deeply immersed in this practice and who has gained realization through it, all appearances, sounds and thoughts are manifestations of Natural Mind. When you are deeply immersed in the practice and it is becoming very stable, you don't lose the strength of it. When that realization remains very strong in your awareness, then whatever forms or sounds or thoughts that appear are the forms of Buddha, sounds of Buddha, thoughts of Buddha.

If you try to write in space, you can't do it, can you? With this kind of realization, if you say something negative, it doesn't create negative karma because you realize it is all empty form. It's like you're writing in empty space. All appearances, all existence, is the emanation of the enlightened body. When you hear negative comments, you are not harmed by them. It creates no suffering. This happens when you realize that everything is the manifestation of the Natural Mind or Dharmakaya.

All events are the play of positive qualities. It is similar for all kinds of activities; they become empty forms. This is the nail of the single sphere, the main point being that all activities, appearances, sounds, and thoughts are within that ultimate, Natural State of Mind. They all emanate within that.

Nail 15

I prostrate to Kuntuzangpo who is without obscurations or karmic tendencies.

In order to completely cut the karmic tendencies of the base-of-all,

Cut the rope of grasping and untie the knots of attachment.

It is taught that when the seeds are eradicated, there will be no return.

The clear and empty sky is the base.

The elements and worldly phenomena are the dynamic energy.

Chasing after them is the way you are deluded.

Viewing them as deficient is the error.

Leaving them as they are is the method.

Freeing them into vastness is the path.

Nonduality is the realization.

Manifesting is the result.

Actionless primordial wisdom is the base.

Varieties of action are the dynamic energy.

Chasing after them is the way you are deluded.

Viewing them as deficient is the error.

Leaving them as they are in the method.

Freeing them into vastness is the path.

Non-duality is the realization.

Manifesting is the result.

Silent primordial wisdom is the base.

Varieties of speech are the dynamic energy.

Chasing after them is the way you are deluded.

Viewing them as deficient is the error.

Leaving them as they are is the method.

Freeing them into vastness is the path.

Non-duality is the realization.

Manifesting is the result.

Thought-free primordial wisdom is the base.

The varieties of thoughts are the dynamic energy.

Chasing after them is the way you are deluded.

Viewing them as deficient is the error.

Leaving them as they are is the method.

Freeing them into vastness is the path.

Non-duality is the realization.

Manifesting is the result.

Self-originated primordial wisdom is the base.

The five poisonous disturbing emotions are the dynamic energy.

Chasing after them is the way you are deluded.

Viewing them as deficient is the error.

Leaving them as they are is the method.

Freeing them into vastness is the path.

Non-duality is the realization.

Manifesting is the result.

The primordial wisdom of innate self-awareness is the base.

Sound, light, and rays are the dynamic energy.

Grasping them as real things is hte way you are deluded.

Viewing them as superior is the error.

Profound certainty is the method. Freeing them into their own appearance is the path.

The absence of their self-nature is the realizaiton.

Arising as dynamic energy is the result.

This completes the nail of profound certainty, [the unification of] mother and son.

Samaya!

This nail is an important one because it discusses the kinds of mistakes we can make in our practice. There is usage of the terms, mother and child, with mother referring to the Ultimate Nature itself, and the child referring to the appearances that arise from it. We make prostrations to Kuntuzangpo with the understanding that the Ultimate Nature and appearances are like mother and child. With that kind of understanding there is no possibility of deception occurring. When we are aware that appearances arise from the Natural State, there is no ignorance or deception. The factor of ignorance in our mind can be removed; it is adventitious and temporary. It is with this understanding that Ultimate Nature and appearances are like a mother and child, that we make prostration to Kuntuzangpo.

We meditate on Natural Mind or the essential nature of the mind in order to cut through karmic traces and to cut through the knots of attachment until they can no longer arise.

There are some brief statements made here about how

meditation should go as well as mistakes that can be made. The text speaks of base, path and result. At the base is a union of emptiness and awareness, which is like empty sky. Then, the elements of the universe are like the dynamic energy of Natural Mind. By following after appearances, whether during meditation or on other occasions, we are deceived. To think that these appearances are something to be gotten rid of, however, is a wrong turn, a mistaken direction.

The method is to leave them just as they are. Whenever appearances arise, rather than thinking that it is wrong or that it shouldn't be happening, the method is just to leave them be. The path is releasing them in emptiness. The Tibetan word, *long (long)*, expanse or space, is being used here to refer to the emptiness; releasing appearances to emptiness is the path. The realization is a nonduality. When you realize that appearances are not separate from Natural Mind, this is the realization. Whenever someone realizes this, whether in or out of meditation, that is the resultant state. There are many words describing this particular nail, but they are all describing the same point. The pattern is the same: the base, the manifestation of energy, how we are deceived, the wrong turn that could be taken, the method to be used, the path, the manifestation, and the result. These repeat using various metaphors.

Actionless primordial wisdom is the base. Transcendent wisdom is free of activity. What is meant by being free of action primarily refers to being free of intellectual mind, free of subject/object conceptuality. The varieties of action, the thoughts of the mind, are the energy of Natural Mind manifesting. The remaining statements follow the same pattern: chasing after these manifestations is how you are deluded, viewing them as deficient is the error, leaving them as they are is the method, freeing them into vastness is the path, non-duality is the realization, and manifestation of that is the result.

As for all of the practices, like deity visualization, recitation of mantra and so on, you don't abandon them, but on the other hand, they are not to be grasped. It is similar to when we meditate, we don't intentionally try to stop thinking. And yet, when thoughts arise, we don't follow them. This is a path of release, a liberating path. Whether we are meditating or engaged in any activity, these are all viewed in the same way.

The next set says that base is inexpressible transcendent wisdom and the various expressions of speech are its manifestations. The pattern is the same. If we chase after words, that's how we are deceived. If we see them as faulty, that is a wrong turn. Letting them be is the method, releasing them in emptiness is the path, nonduality is the realization, and manifestation is the result.

The following set says that the basis is non-conceptual transcendent wisdom. If we are meditating in Natural Mind, all thinking is left to subside. Thought-free Primordial Wisdom is the basis. The various thoughts that arise are its manifestations. Following after them is how we are deceived. Trying to stop them is the mistaken direction. Everything else is the same.

The next stanza speaks of the basis as being Self-Arising Transcendent Wisdom within the two aspects of Natural

Mind—self-arising and self-knowing. Deluded states of mind—the five poisons of ignorance, attachment, aversion, jealousy and pride—are nothing other than the energy of Natural Mind arising. There is no need to get involved with them, chase after them, stop them, see them as faulty. That's the way we are deceived.

There are different approaches to these five delusions in different aspects of the teachings. In the context of sutra they are referred to as five poisonous delusions and, as such, need to be eliminated, purified, washed away; if they are not, we have a problem. Thus, in the system of sutra, they are seen as something to be abandoned.

In the general tantric teachings, the five poisons are not seen as something to be abandoned, but rather something that can be transformed. The five delusions can be transformed into the five transcendent wisdoms. The general tantric teachings are known as the Path of Transformation. In the Dzogchen way, the five poisons don't need to be abandoned, nor do they need to be transformed. It is a path of release, of letting go. Here, seeing them as faulty is a wrong turn. Letting them be is the method, and seeing them as empty is the path.

In the final section, the basis is the self-knowing primordial wisdom. The awareness side of Natural Mind and its manifestations arise as subtle sounds, lights, and rays. The way they are described is therefore a little different than in the previous stanzas. Perceiving these subtle visions as real or truly existent is the way we are deceived. Viewing them as supreme is the error, the wrong turn. These visions may even be of Buddhas, mandalas or pure lands. Our lamas advise us, even if that happens, do not think it is great. Don't get all excited about it; if you do, that's an error. In this case the method is deep certainty—certainty that they are manifestations of the Natural State and not arising from something outside. Seeing them as appearances of the Natural State and releasing them is the path. Whether they are subtle or gross appearances, realize that they are just like waves of the ocean—they arise out of Natural Mind, they never go beyond it, and they dissolve back into it; this is the path on which they are released. The realization is that those subtle sounds, lights, and rays are not inherently existent; they lack self-nature, they are manifestations of the Natural State. Seeing these subtle appearances arise as the energy of the Natural State is the result. This is not to say that this is the ultimate result of practice; it is a result that a person who is practicing experiences.

Nail 16

I prostrate to Kuntuzangpo, the non-abiding perfection.

The space of the base-of-all does not fall into bias or partiality.

The primordial wisdom of innate awareness is beyond expression and action.

The reflecting intellect is without base or cessation.

Sound, light, and rays are without attachment and anger.

Do not cling to the defiled as inferior or the undefiled as superior.

Do not view purity as a positive quality or impurity as a fault.

Samsara and nirvana are inseparable and cannot be divided.

Buddhas and sentient beings are nondual and are indistinguishable.

You can neither enter nor progress on the path of innate awareness.

In bodhicitta there are neither vehicles nor philosophies.

In the state of equanimity there is neither good nor bad, neither high nor low.

This completes the nail of transcendent equanimity.

Samaya!

In the sixteenth nail, the nail of equality, there is prostration to Kuntuzangpo who does not abide in that which has gone beyond. Saying that Kuntuzangpo does not abide means that Kuntuzangpo does not abide in samsara or nirvana, because the basis-of-all, the Natural State, pervades all of samsara and nirvana. General sutra teachings speak of going beyond samsara or getting out of samsara. In Dzogchen teachings, there is emphasis on going beyond both samsara and nirvana. So we prostrate to Kuntuzangpo Dharmakaya with the understanding that it does not abide in either samsara or nirvana. This is primarily showing that within the ultimate nature of the Natural State there is no difference between samsara and nirvana; they are the same.

The space of the base-of-all does not fall into bias or partiality. Natural Mind, the base-of-all, pervades everywhere without partiality. It is not present in some places and absent in others. It is not cut off, nor is there extra. Rather, all of samsara and nirvana can arise within it. It is like space; either white or dark clouds can arise.

All the elements of earth, water, fire and so on—can arise within space. It pervades all.

Self-knowing primordial wisdom is without analysis and is inexpressible. No sort of thinking can effect it. It doesn't change or improve. Whether it's a valid inference or not, no conceptual mind effects primordial transcendent wisdom. Whether you use a lot of words or just a few words, whether you use words that are very eloquent or plain words, whether it is Buddha talking or a normal sentient being talking, no words can touch or explain what it is.

Do we cease all thinking when meditation in the Natural State? No, thoughts can arise. They are allowed to arise. However, these thoughts are not findable; when we seek them out, they lack any foundation. When you identify them, they lead back to nothing but the Natural State. The actual mode of existence of the mind has nothing supporting it; it is baseless. Whether it's the subtle appearances of the light, rays and sounds, or the grosser appearances of form, sound, sights, tastes, and so on, whether they're pleasant or unpleasant, whether they give rise to attraction or aversion—no matter what, they are all lacking their own self-basis. They all lead back to that ultimate nature, Natural Mind. They can't be found. They are baseless. Whether they're good or bad, they're all the same in lacking any self-foundation. In ultimate nature, whether contaminated or uncontaminated by ignorance, it's all the same. In that ultimate nature there is no difference between purity and impurity. Like clean water compared to dirty water; they are both water. When you have realization of the Natural State, you really don't find any difference between samsara and nirvana. In that ultimate nature, there is no difference between Buddhas and sentient beings; awakened beings are not better and sentient beings are not worse.

In Natural Mind, there is no engaging with logic or moving along a path of logic. So analyzing with thought, logic, or valid perception has no place in the Natural State. Likewise, passing through the different paths of accumulation, preparation, seeing, meditation, and no more learning—these are all paths designated by thought, created by the conceptual mind. In the ultimate state, there is no engaging the path through conceptual thinking or passing through conceptual stages.

In bodhicitta, there are no tenets or vehicles. Here, in the mind of enlightenment, *jang chub kyi sem (byang chub kyi sems),* bodhicitta refers to Natural Mind, the actual way things exist, the most essential mind; and so it is referring to ultimate bodhicitta. In ultimate bodhicitta, there are no tenet systems, because tenet systems are philosophies devised by a thinking, logical mind which conceives ideas of how things exist: this is correct, this is incorrect, and so forth. Within the ultimate nature of mind, there is no place for that. The vehicles are conceived by a conceptual mind, as well; none of them exist within the Natural State. They abide in equality; they are equal. There is no better or worse understanding in Natural Mind. There is a discussion of something like a tenet system in this teaching but, in the Natural State itself, none of that exists. In philosophical terms, how we describe, perceive things, or determine where we are in a process of realization—these kinds of perceptions do not exist in the Natural State. In our daily lives the pleasant and unpleasant feelings that we experience are also the energy of the Natural State manifesting. Realizing this acts as a remedy to all suffering that arises.

This nail primarily shows that, once we are firmly resolved within the understanding of Natural Mind, all of these varieties are equal.

Nail 17

I prostrate to Kuntuzangpo, the body of the ultimate king.

The worldly phenomena of the four elements dissolve into the space of the sky.

The vehicles, lineages, and doors of bon dissolve into the space of the nature of bon.

The mind and mental states dissolve into the space of the nature of mind.

The varieties of activities dissolve into the space of stillness.

The varieties of speech dissolve into the space of silence.

The clouds of thoughts and recollections dissolve into the space free of thought.

Sound, light, and rays dissolve into the space of innate awareness.

Nirvana and samsara completely dissolve into bodhicitta.

All paths fabricated by the intellect dissolve into the space beyond intellect.

Philosophies and biases dissolve into the space beyond bias.

Appearances do not dissolve, stop, or cease.

The original source and ultimate liberation blend here—

Neither dissolving nor ceasing, continuous in the three times.

This completes the nail of reaching the ultimate dissolution.

Samaya!

Next we have prostration to Kuntuzangpo, the Ultimate King. With conceptual mind, we can talk about such things as relative and ultimate truths. In this context we can think of Natural Mind as ultimate truth and the manifestations that arise from it as conventional truth. When we penetrate appearances of conventional truths, they lead us back to the Natural State. Here we prostrate to Kuntuzangpo as king of the knowledge that conventional truths lead back to ultimate truth. The example given in the text is that whatever arises in space—the elements, clouds, rain—when you seek them out you find nothing but the sphere of space itself.

This nail speaks of the exhaustion of things, how things are finished in the ultimate state. Whatever philosophies, tenet systems, vehicles are used to view the practice of the teachings, when they are followed, they ultimately disappear into Natural Mind. Mind and mental factors are also exhausted in the essential nature of the mind. However we enumerate consciousnesses, whether as six with five sense consciousness and one mental consciousness, or eight with the addition of deluded mind and mind-basis-of-all, all of these are exhausted within the essential Natural Mind, the Natural State.

When we engage in various actions of body, speech and mind, whether they are positive or negative in nature, in the ultimate state they are exhausted. The nature of the ultimate state is a sphere of no activity. Likewise, expressions, nice or not, dharmic or not, when you trace their source to the ultimate state, they disappear. Natural Mind is an expressionless, free state with no words.

Concepts disappear in the Natural State. There are many varieties of conceptual thought. For instance, someone who has been to Tibet has direct perceptions of it. But if you've never been to Tibet, all you can do is think about it, have some sort of image in your mind. These are gross forms of conceptual thought. There are also subtler types of conceptual thought, such as conceptions of things as self-existent. Whatever concepts they are, however, when they dissolve in the Natural State, it is a state that is thought free, a state where thoughts don't exist.

All paths are exhausted in the Natural State. Some texts speak of good paths that lead to nirvana and bad paths that lead to samsara. Because Natural Mind is a state beyond conceptual thought, paths which involve such thinking, whether good or bad, disappear in the ultimate state.

There is no partiality in the Natural State. When tenet systems are discussed or debated one practitioner might say "My guru says this, this is how things are, this is how things exist." Another practitioner, holding a different position, might think "they've fallen to an extreme; they've taken a wrong direction." This kind of partisanship is exhausted in the Natural State. Natural Mind is a state which pervades all, impartially. Before practitioners realize the Natural State, they can practice whatever tenet system they like because it doesn't make any difference; it all arises from and dissolves into the Natural State. With that kind of understanding of the ultimate, we can really be nonpartisan—what we call *rimé (ris med)* in Tibetan.

Also, the subtle appearances of sounds, lights and rays

dissolve into the Natural State. When, through thögel practice, subtle visions are caused to appear as one reaches high levels of realization, they then disappear. In this way, we rely upon the signs dissolving into the Natural State. Those subtle visions that appear are signs of the Natural State and they lead back to the Natural State where they disappear.

All of samsara and nirvana are exhausted in ultimate bodhicitta, Natural Mind. All of the states of samsara and nirvana become like the moon reflected in water; they are exhausted in the Natural State. The metaphor of the moon being reflected in water means that they are leading back to the Natural State, the essence of mind. They are exhausted.

The text states that appearances dissolve but they do not cease. The ultimate point of their arising and the ultimate point of their ceasing meet in the Natural State, the essence of mind; in general, they do not come to an end. Whether they are subtle appearances of lights, sounds and rays, or grosser appearances of sights, sounds, and so forth, they disappear in the Natural State and also arise out of it. The environment and living beings, their minds and mental factors do not come to an end, there is no cessation of them. The ultimate state is not exhausted; it exists throughout the three times, constantly throughout the past, present or future. It is the same for both macrocosm or microcosm. The external world dissolves into the Natural State and arises out of it. Likewise, when we are meditating, thoughts arise from the Natural State and dissolve back into it.

Nail 18

I prostrate to Kuntuzangpo, compassionate protector of beings.

At the end [of this life], at the time when body and mind separate,

At the junction of comfort and misery,

For the person of superior intelligence,

The quintessential instruction of self-arising primordial wisdom is taught.

The instruction of the equality of the various [appearances] is conferred.

Without a doubt you see your own face.

For the person of average intelligence,

*The quintessential instruction
of illusory self-appearance is taught.*

Given the instruction of no desire or attachment,

Without a doubt the door to rebirth is closed.

For the person of lesser intelligence,

*The quintessential instruction of the master
and deity is taught.*

Once the instruction of earnest devotion is conferred,

Without a doubt a comfortable birthplace is obtained.

This completes the nail of generating bodhicitta at the time of death.

Samaya!

The text of the eighteenth nail begins, homage to Kuntuzangpo who protects migrating beings with compassion. The Natural State of Kuntuzangpo Dharmakaya within us has the power to protect living beings. If we recognize Natural Mind and practice it, this has the power to protect us at the time of death when our body and mind separate. In the course of our daily life, the Natural State of Kuntuzangpo, has the power to protect us. As we find that appearances are not truly existent they continue to dissolve back into our mind. The extent to which Natural Mind protects us depends upon the extent of our understanding and practice of it. If we practice every day and gradually increase our experience, it will increasingly have the power to protect us.

The eighteenth nail discusses practices and guidance that should be given to a person at the time of death, depending upon their level of faculties: highest, middling, or lesser.

A person of highest faculties is taught the instruction on self-arising primordial wisdom and the equality of appearances, and as a result, they will see their own face, their own true nature, without doubt. These are the instructions you have been reading. The instructions on Natural Mind and appearances are not different; in fact, they are inseparable. If the person is a practitioner, they have a chance to greatly benefit at this time. The extent to which they are introduced to this guidance and have awareness of the Natural State will make a big difference in what comes after death, in the bardo, the intermediate state.

For someone of mid-level faculties who haven't had tremendous experience of Dzogchen meditation, but neither are they the least experienced—the instructions given at the time of death are "Now your are dying. Whatever appears to you will be illusory." In this way they will be given instructions that do not directly point to the Natural State itself, but close to it. Appearances that arise are illusory, not found to be truly self-existent. They are also given the instruction not to be attached to anything: the body they have cherished so dearly in life, their residence, their property, their enjoyment of sights and sounds they've experienced. They are instructed not to crave any of these things.

In the case of a person of lesser faculties, who has had some practice or experience, they are instructed to remember their guru and the instructions they have received from them, to develop conviction and devotion to the guru, and to pray and aspire to realize the guru's teachings. They are reminded of the guru from whom they have received teachings throughout their life.

There is a story about a Bön master name Ponse Chunggo Tsal in the 11th century. He had a vision of hell while he was alive because of some previous karma. He went unconscious for a while and saw fires, cauldrons, and other frightening things. He had visions of hellish realms of existence. At the beginning he was afraid of the visions, but immediately remembering the instructions he had received from his guru about hell being a manifestation of the Natural State, he absorbed himself in the Natural State and the vision of hell disappeared.

After he woke he told his disciples of the experience, illustrating how understanding of the Natural State can protect you.

When these instructions are given to a dying person, it can benefit them in these ways. Depending on the extent of practice, it can at best be full awakening or enlightenment; at a middling level, it can bring rebirth with high status; at least, it can ensure precious human rebirth. This concludes the nail called bodhicitta at the time of death.'

Nail 19

I prostrate to Kuntuzangpo, the self-liberated, complete Buddha.

As to instruction regarding the time of delusion and liberation:

The outer elements fall apart [and dissolve] into their own place.

The inner elements are dormant.

Conceptions of subject and object are absorbed into vastness.

At that time, innate awareness nakedly abides.

Self-originated primordial wisdom is uncovered.

Some fortunate ones who possess profound certainty

*Break the three seals and then
complete the three dynamic energies.*

*If you are not liberated by that,
Then the first bardo arises.*

Lights [form] a pure realm without boundaries.

They arise like a rainbow in the sky.

Sound is insubstantial and roars in the vastness.

It is unceasing and self-originated like the sound of a dragon.

Rays display an unpredictable magical illusion.

They billow open like silk brocade.

For the person who is accustomed and familiar,

Bodies and mandalas arise in their completeness.

At that time, through the recollections and clairvoyances,

The three appearances arise as hostesses.

Escorted by your own familiarity,

Your mind stream of innate awareness arrives at the base.

You see appearances as your own face

Like seeing your face reflected in a mirror.

Your innate self-awareness meets itself

Like recognizing a prince.

Deluded ignorance naturally clears

Like the sun shining in a dark place.

The king of innate awareness arrives at his own place

Like a prince taking his throne.

Sound, light, and rays are purified in the mind
Like the sun's rays are collected in the sun.
The impure is liberated in the vastness of the pure
Like ice melting in the ocean.
Defilements are pacified in the state of the undefiled
Like salt dissolving in water.
Karma and mental afflictions are liberated in the base
Like masses of clouds dispersing in the sky.
The three realms of samsara are shaken from their depths
Like a river dried up at its source.
Nirvana and samsara are purified in the nondual base
Like rainbows disappearing in the sky.
The three bodies spontaneously arise
Like the rays of the sun or moonlight [reflecting] on water.
For persons of little familiarity,
The king of innate awareness lies dormant.
Abiding [in the base-of-all] from one to three [days],
The pure [lights] gradually dawn in seven [days].
[If] the pure realm does not completely appear,

[Even so] through [the right] causal conditions you [may yet be] liberated in the bardo.

If you are not liberated, gross appearances dawn.

In the bardo of existence you see pure appearances,

And if you are repeatedly born in good circumstances, you can be quickly liberated.

Those persons without the door of instruction

Do not recognize the Natural State even though it is clear.

Seeing appearances as external and true,

They enter the snare of delusion and wander in samsara.

Therefore, the fortunate achieve profound certainty.

This completes the nail of the time of the bardo.

Samaya!

This next nail goes into more depth about the intermediate state, the *bardo (bar do)*, and the means of obtaining liberation in the intermediate state.

I prostrate to Kuntuzangpo, self-liberated, fully en-lightened Buddha. Just as we speak of the Natural State being self-arisen, it is also self-released. When we meditate, we are meditating on the self-released Natural State. Because appearances arise out of the Natural State, abide in the Natural State, and dissolve back into the Natural State, we say that they are self-liberated. There is no thought, logic, or thinking process involved. There are no valid perceptions or inferences that must be developed. Therefore, it is said to be self-liberated. In other scriptures, it is explained that if, for instance, anger or hatred arises, then you need to develop something else to put in its place as a remedy: patience or love. Here, it is not like that. Anger, by just being seen and allowed to dissolve back into the Natural State, requires no other remedy, it is self-liberated. The main reason that anger and other mental afflictions are self-liberated is that they have no foundation, they are baseless. The term 'fully enlightened' is also used to describe the Natural State.

As to instructions regarding the time of delusion and liberation:

The outer elements fall apart [and dissolve] into their own place.

The inner elements are dormant.

Conceptions of subject and object are absorbed into vastness.

The outer and inner elements cease to function, the body is dropped and ceases to obscure Natural Mind. At the time of death when the elements dissolve and the Natural State nakedly shines forth, obscurations drop away and a person can attain enlightenment at that very moment. We say that the ultimate state itself is fully enlightened, but if a person hasn't realized that, they are not fully enlightened. At this point, when the obscurations of the elements disintegrate, a person at the highest level of practice can obtain full awakening, Buddhahood. If their practice has not developed sufficiently and they do not attain enlightenment, then the bardo experience dawns.

Visions of lights, rays and sound will appear. There is a very strong radiant light that appears—an appearance of a very luminous realm of existence—like rainbows arising in the sky with brilliant light. Then sounds will arise—very loud sounds like thunder in the sky. Rays of various types will appear in all sorts of shapes—square, oval, round, varicolored rays of light like bright, colored fabrics.

To a person who has been deeply immersed in the practice, these rays will appear as enlightened beings, Buddha realms, awakened beings and mandalas, pure lands and so on. It's very important at this point to remember the instructions that you have received from your teacher. If you can remember the instructions, then remember how all of these appearances exist within the Natural State.

In other scriptures, we talk about the realization of appearances to be like reflections in a mirror. When you have experiences of Natural Mind, you realize that they are like reflections in a mirror and what you're seeing is originating from yourself. It is arising from yourself and you can also see it. It is like a prince who has escaped from the palace and is masquerading as an ordinary person. People are looking and not realizing it at first, but eventually realize that it's the prince. Appearances are recognized as emanating from the Natural State. Ignorance is gone, like the sun rising in the sky to clear away the darkness. In this way, appearances are understood to be manifestations of Natural Mind. The subtle visions of light, rays and sounds are understood to be the nature of the Natural State, just like rays of the sun are understood to be from the sun. All impure phenomena dissolves into the Natural State. Appearances are like ice in water; when there is a warmer environment, the ice melts back into the water and can no longer be differentiated from the water. Like that, appearances dissolve back into the Natural State.

All contaminated and uncontaminated phenomena are like salt; when placed in water it dissolves and can no longer be found or differentiated. No matter how thick we've been with delusions and karma, it all dissolves into the Natural State. No matter how densely gathered clouds are, they eventually dissipate and disappear. The three realms of samsaric existence—desire, form and formless realms, all evaporate and disappear, like a river that has been cut off at the source and ceases to flow. Samsara and nirvana are realized to be equal when they dissolve like rainbows disappearing in the sky. The ultimate state has this spontaneously accomplished quality. Remember that all the qualities of realization are spontaneously accomplished within Natural Mind. Mandalas of the three bodies of Buddha will naturally arise within it, like the rays coming from the sun or the moon reflected in water. Those with a middling level of accomplishment will have these kinds of experiences.

If a person is of lesser faculties and has not recognized the Natural State, it will remain dormant within them; there will be an indeterminate number of days that they will remain in the intermediate state. Over a period of about seven weeks the person in the intermediate state will continue to have various kinds of visions and appearances that arise. There will be appearances of Buddhas and mandalas, but incomplete; they will be in partial form. But again, if the person is able to remember, at any point, the instructions they have received, then there is still the possibility that they may be liberated into the Natural State. If they don't attain liberation at that time, they will enter the *Si pe bardo (Srid p'i bardo)* of existence, another life. Even at that point, if they can recall the instructions they have received, they may be able to take a fortunate human rebirth.

If someone has not recognized the Natural State, has not practiced it, or has received instructions but has not applied them in practice, they will continue to grasp the appearances that arise as truly existent, as coming from outside themselves, and continue to be deceived. It would be like the people in the example who did not recognize the prince and just thought that he was an ordinary person. They will not recognize their visions or appearances as coming from the king, Natural Mind. Regardless of whether someone has practiced and realized it or not, the Natural State will appear to them, but they will not be able to recognize it and will take rebirth in the process that is extensively described in the *12 Links of Interdependent Origination*.

This nail concludes by saying that the fortunate should achieve profound certainty. What is being emphasized here is that the time of transition in the intermediate state is of profound importance and will make the difference between attaining liberation and awakening or continuing to wander in deluded suffering. Understanding that this is the critical point, someone who has received these instructions should, with deep certainty, put them into practice. The practice we do during our life is the very same practice that we will do in the time of transition. This completes the nail of the bardo.

Nail 20

I prostrate to Kuntuzangpo, dispeller of the darkness of misconceptions.

If this instruction of the ultimate vital point

Is taught to those unable to handle it,

Such as those lacking fortune or karmic links,

Some will hold these [appearances of sound, light, and rays] as [an eternal] self

And stray into the heretical position of eternalism.

Some will say "There are no appearances,"

And stray into the position of nihilism.

Some will cling to this as supreme

And stray into eternalism of long-lived [gods].

Some will regard this with an arrogant mind

And will be shackled in the chains of their own egotistical knowledge.

Some will hold to this as substantial

And will be bound in samsara through their attachment to substantiality.

Some will have fear and apprehension toward this.

These less intelligent ones will stray into the lower vehicles.

Some will belittle this

And will delay meeting the benefit for eons.

Some will feel this instruction is just crazy activity

And will fall to lower births through this degeneration of samaya.

In these ways it is a steep cliff.

Therefore, this holy quintessential instruction

Should be hidden as a treasure in the mind, the base-of-all.

Do not spread it; seal it with secrecy.

This completes the nail of dispelling the extreme misconceptions.

Samaya!

Nail nineteen continues with the instructions: I prostrate to Kuntuzangpo, dispeller of the darkness of misconceptions. When we are introduced to the Natural State, have practiced and developed experience of it, it clears away mistaken ideas. We prostrate to Kuntuzangpo with the understanding that, by absorbing ourself in the Natural State, it will clear away all of our misconceptions. In effect, this is saying that we need to have a correct understanding of absorption into the Natural State in order to clear away mistaken ideas about it. The Natural State is free from mistaken extremes. Whether extremes are classified into 8, 4, or 2 categories, realization of the ultimate nature dispels all of them. Some of these extremes are extremes of nihilism, of permanence, of existence, of non-existence, of appearances, and of emptiness. It is difficult to understand that which is free from all of these extremes. It is best, therefore, to keep this teaching somewhat secret and confidential.

Appearances that are connected with thinking and concepts arise to us and we tend to follow after them.

When we cling to appearances and chase after them, it obstructs our understanding of Natural Mind. Therefore, if this teaching is given to someone who is not ripe for it, they can't really understand it. It is similar to the story of when Buddha attained enlightenment and discovered a dharma that was like nectar—the clear light mind of the Natural State. At first he felt it was so profound and subtle, that it would be difficult for anyone to understand and that he should just keep it to himself and meditate in the jungle. He remained there for seven weeks, until Indra and Brahma visited, offered him the conch and golden dharma wheel and requested teachings. The period Buddha kept it secret is similar to this; it was so profound that he thought there could be a danger of people misunderstanding.

One of the dangers when these instructions are given to someone is that they make the mistake of giving the Natural State a supposed true mode of existence. This is a big problem because, when someone grasps the ultimate nature as being truly existent this is the exact opposite of the reality, which is its interdependent origination. Understanding the Natural State is the foundation for going on to understanding interdependent origination.

Others make the mistake of thinking that none of these appearances actually exist, that Buddhas, mandalas, and any other appearances that arise are completely non-existent, thus falling into a completely nihilistic view, an extreme of nihilism. This denies the spontaneously accomplished quality in which all things can and do arise. They don't understand that there is both an empty quality as well as an aware nature in Natural Mind.

Some might hold the Natural State to be absolutely supreme and concretize it, similar to a creator god, thinking that the whole world is created out of it. They externalize it and don't realize it is within themselves. This misunderstanding can cause rebirth in one of the god realms, trapped in samsara. Some people, upon hearing these teachings, might develop pride in knowledge of them without actually applying them in practice. Another mistake that can be made is to conceive of the practice, the appearances and so forth, as truly existent. This clinging to the reality of it will cause further wandering in the suffering of cyclic existence.

Some others, when given these instructions, become terrified by them. They become frightened and confused by the explanation of samsara and nirvana being equal, and tend to revert back to lesser vehicles; i.e., teachings in which a distinction is made between samsara and nirvana, and samsara is to be abandoned.

In the practice of the general tantric teachings, deity yoga for instance, great effort is put into actualizing the nature of the deity through growth of realization and the recitation of mantras. In Dzogchen practice such effort is not applied. That would be a result of not having full conviction in the Dzogchen teachings, not really believing that the deities and mandalas spontaneously arise within the Natural State and believing that you have to work at it to realize the deity.

When Dzogchen is presented to them, some feel that it

is a denial of things that do validly exist. They feel that it's slanderous or blasphemous of things that do exist, that it is a denial of Buddhist teachings. If they hold these teachings in disdain, it will take eons of time before they encounter such teachings again.

Some people give these instructions incorrectly, thus breaking their bond with the teachings and guru. This can result in rebirth in worse realms of existence, hells and so on. That is why this teaching should be kept confidential; it could present such danger for people who would misunderstand it. Whatever you have understood should be kept in your mind, not exposing it.

This nail is mainly concerned with dispelling extremes and misconceptions about the Natural State and these instructions because of the danger of people not understanding, misunderstanding, or partially understanding and making mistakes.

Guru Yoga is considered most important for aiding development of correct understanding. Here, Guru

Yoga focuses on the Kuntuzangpo aspect. The ultimate source of these teachings is Kuntuzangpo Dharmakaya. Inseparable from Kuntuzangpo, the teachings spread to Sambhogakaya and Nirmanakaya forms, and to the human recipients, masters of the lineage. When we recognize and rest in Natural Mind, this is, in fact, Guru Yoga. We make many prostrations to Guru Kuntuzangpo; when we realize it is the essence of our very own nature, this conjoins us with Guru Yoga.

The Natural State is difficult to understand, and that is why there are multiple approaches in the nine different vehicles. They are all approaching the ultimate meaning, getting closer and closer to understanding Natural Mind, but not quite getting there. Like blind men trying to describe an elephant, one grabs the tail and says the elephant is like a snake; another might touch the elephant's ear and say that the elephant is more like the leaf of a tree, and so on. They are all getting some understanding, but its not complete. All the vehicles are meant to approach understanding of the Natural State. It's not easy to understand. It all depends on how sharp a person's faculties are. Or you might say it depends on how much positive energy or merit a person has accumulated.

Sometimes, when people first hear these teachings, they will not understand them, but by applying them and putting them into practice, they gradually develop an understanding. They may become a person of sharper faculties with more wisdom. That is why, in the Nyingma and Bön traditions, there are nine vehicles explained. These are levels of philosophy that help one refine the grosser factors, then become more subtle and profound as they ascend. The understanding of those lower levels of philosophy serves as a foundation for understanding the higher levels.

Dawa Drakpa, disciple of Shardza Rinpoche who attained the rainbow body, said that understanding Madhyamaka, the Middle Way teachings, had aided his understanding of Dzogchen. It was the Middle Way teachings about appearances of mind not being truly existent, not having their own separate, independent existence.

When perceived as having such existence, when an appearance seems attractive, it is overemphasized and given inappropriate attention. This promotes a sense that there is an object there, something to be clung to. In attachment, there is not the slightest awareness of how the attractive object arose from causes and conditions and is dependent upon its parts and aspects; it just seems to be there, distinct, existing from its own side.

The Madhyamaka teachings analyze objects of mind, revealing how their appearance as independently existent is mistaken. Our believing in the truth of that appearance is also mistaken. The main reason given is because objects are interdependent, meaning dependent upon other factors. In Dzogchen, there is no attention paid to emptiness of inherent existence of objects; rather they are all viewed as the empty mind's energy arising. In Dzogchen teachings, the single understanding of the Natural State and its emptiness extends to and pervades the emptiness of all phenomena. It is quite convenient in that all you need to focus on is Natural Mind rather than the emptiness of inherent existence of all the various objects.

Dzogchen is a path of release. We realize that all phenomena are manifestations of the Natural State. Our understanding extends to all other phenomena because we see that they have all arisen out of the Natural State like waves of the ocean, rising and dissolving back. In this way, it's not necessary to understand the emptiness of many different objects. Simply understand the emptiness of Natural Mind. It is said to all be understood within a single sphere. It's because of not having the understanding of that emptiness of Natural Mind, that there are other modes of presentation within Buddhist teachings. The many different scriptures written by great masters clarifying various tenet systems have all been the result of their different approaches, their attempts to understand the ultimate nature and explain it to others. For example, out of the three rounds of Dharma that Buddha taught, there are even differences of opinion as to whether Buddha's ultimate, definitive teachings were given in the second or the third round of his teachings.

It all comes down to different ways of presenting the ultimate nature from the Dzogchen perspective of Natural Mind. Remember the thumb-sized Dharmakaya. It pertains to the single sphere of all in one—emptiness, awareness, wisdom and skillful means—all are included in this single sphere.

Nail 21

I prostrate to Kuntuzangpo who manifests the three bodies.

Through a profound certainty in the ultimate meaning,
These results will emerge without a doubt.

Through a profound certainty in the base-of-all,
nirvana and samsara are swept away.

Through a profound certainty in innate awareness,
deluded obscurations [are realized to be] primordially pure.

Through a profound certainty about [the Natural State of] the intellect, the dynamic energy of primordial wisdom arises.

Through a profound certainty about the base of delusion, innate awareness is irreversible.

Through the dissolution of mental afflictions, the current of samsara is cut.

Through the dissolution of the paths, the state of great bliss is achieved.

Through the dissolution of philosophy, there is no bias regarding your own and others' positions.

Through the dissolution of the elements, there is no diminishing of the sky.

Through the dissolution of the attributes, there is no change in space.

Through the dissolution of sentient beings, there is no birth and death in the mind.

Through the dissolution of the three doors, the three dynamic energies are complete in the body.

Through the dissolution of the three appearances, the three aspects of the mandala arise.

Because the two spaces arise in you, bliss abides in the bon nature.

Because the two lights arise in you, bliss does not wane.

Because of arising as the unceasing-unchanging body, you are separated from the enemy of discomfort.

Because the six eyes arise in you, nothing obscures you.

Because the three bodies arise in you, you have neither hope nor fear of the result.

Because the door to the treasure of the mind is opened, everything you need is complete within you.

This completes the nail of manifesting the result.

Samaya!

I prostrate to Kuntuzangpo who manifests the three bodies. This is the nail of Kuntuzangpo who manifests. Having recognized the Natural State and having practiced it, our understanding will develop and grow. In the Natural State itself, however, there is no growth. The three resultant bodies of Buddha are already present in it. With that recognition, we prostrate to Kuntuzangpo.

This nail has to do with the kinds of results that will arise if we have experience of Natural Mind and develop deep certainty in this practice. Once we develop this deep certainty, all hope for nirvana and fear of samsara are swept away. All deception, delusion, and obscuration is purified. As appearances arise, rather than seeing them as truly existent, we see them as if they were drawings in space. They are empty so they can no longer obscure understanding of the Natural State. We are no longer deceived by them. When we no longer pursue appearances and conceptual thought, we are not obscured by them. This allows self-knowing wisdom to shine forth. At that point, we never leave awareness of the Natural State. We never turn away from it or part from it.

We all develop delusions of attachment and aversion and they can become very dense. But when delusions are released into the Natural State, the river of samsara dries up. As we complete the path, whether it is the path presented in sutra, the general tantras, or Dzogchen, we reach a state of great bliss. As philosophies and tenet systems are exhausted and released in realization of the Natural State, all kinds of prejudices and biases disappear. We no longer hold any philosophy, dharma tradition, or spiritual path as better than others.

Through dissolution of the elements, there is no diminishing of the sky. As we understand the Natural State, it doesn't change. Clouds and rainbows appear in the sky; they eventually dissolve, but the sky remains. When an appearance dissolves into the Natural State, it doesn't disappear; it remains eternally.

Through dissolution of the attributes, there is no change in space. With the exhaustion of signs and attributes, concepts about them and words describing them, doesn't change the sphere of space.

In the dissolution of sentient beings, there is no birth and death in the Mind. In the context of these Dzogchen teachings, a sentient being is trapped in samsara because of not understanding Natural Mind, and instead, objectifies and chases after appearances that arise. A Buddha is someone who realizes Natural Mind, who does not chase after appearances but, in fact, gains control of appearances by understanding their source. When that happens, it is the end of being a sentient being; they will never again take birth through the force of delusions and karma. There is no more birth and death for them as a sentient being. In saying that a being is no longer born, this does not mean that they cease to exist. When they realize the Natural State, a spontaneous accomplishment of the Buddhas and mandalas naturally arises. These will arise like the moon reflected in a body of water. It is not the end of existence; it is just the end of birth and death through the force of karma and delusion.

Through the dissolution of the three doors, the three dynamic energies are complete in the body. Normally, when we act with body, speech or mind, it involves effort. When effortful actions of body, speech and mind dissolve in the Natural State, the three dynamic bodies of the Buddhas naturally arise, spontaneously and effortlessly. Being effortless is an important idea in Dzogchen. From the Dzogchen point of view, the striving involved in reciting hundreds of thousands of mantras of a deity comes from one not really believing Dzogchen or not believing that things can be spontaneously accomplished just through realizing the essence of mind, the Natural State. Therefore, Dzogchen meditation is to be undertaken without effort. Creating a meditation that does not involve effort leads naturally to the resultant state in which the activities of body, speech and mind in the awakened state are effortless.

Through dissolution of the three appearances, the three aspects of the mandala arise. When release of the subtle appearances, the sounds, rays and lights, has reached its full measure, the three bodies of the Buddhas, mandalas and deities will shine forth.

The two modes of space are the self-arising and self-knowing transcendent wisdom, the emptiness factor and the awareness factor. Because the two spaces arise in you, bliss abides in the bon nature. When these two aspects appear, one realizes the ultimate nature and abides in bliss. One goes beyond suffering and realizes a state of bliss.

As the two lights arise in you, bliss does not wane. Again, the two lights refers to the light of emptiness of Natural Mind and the light of appearances that arise as energy of the Natural State. When these two lights arise in you there is no cessation of you and you experience bliss.

Because of arising as the unceasing-unchanging body, you are separated from the enemy of discomfort. When the *Yungdrung (gyung drung)* body appears you are freed from unpleasant enemies. *Yungdrung*, the Tibetan word for the Sanskrit *swastika*, is a symbol which represents permanence and indestructibility or of being unconquerable. When it manifests within you, there is no destructive force that can affect you. You are unconquerable, freed from opposing forces.

Because the six eyes arise in you, nothing obscures you. These six eyes are not the normal organs of the eyes, but visions present in the enlightened state: eyes of wisdom, eyes of ultimate truth (*the Bon eye*), fleshly eyes (of remote vision), and so forth—six types of clairvoyant eyes that are present in the Natural State. These are realized when you realize the essence of your mind in the Natural State. They cannot be obscured by anything. Everything is manifest and visible.

Because the three bodies arise in you, you have neither hope nor fear of the result. When you manifest the three bodies of Buddha, there is no longer any yearning for enlightenment or fear of rebirth in samsara.

Because the door to the treasure of the mind is opened, everything you need is complete within you. There are two general meanings of the syllable *Dzog* in Dzogchen. One is that everything is finished, but here it means that everything is perfect and complete. All the qualities and facets of enlightenment are perfected and complete.

Epilogue

This is the innermost essence of the tantras, scriptures, and quintessential instructions—

The ultimate path.

The pinnacle of all the vehicles,

This aural transmission lineage of the siddhas,

Is the siddhi of the fortunate.

This completes the nails of the twenty-one vital points.

This has spread from the early mahasiddhas successively through the lineage.

Sarva mangalam!

This section of the teaching is saying that we need to develop the meditation practice within ourselves. Having received this teaching, it is very important that we engage in the practice of Natural Mind and develop experience ourselves, through our own meditation. That is the whole purpose of this teaching.

How to meditate

Meditation instructions:

1) Sit with your spine straight, your neck slightly bent forward. Your eyes not wide open or tightly closed, but slightly open and directed towards the ground in front of you. Breath naturally. Don't hold your mouth tightly closed or wide open; touch the tip of your tongue to the upper palate behind your front teeth to keep from drooling. Feel you are holding neither your mind nor your body very tightly; leave both in a relaxed state.

2) Remember the points of posture: your spine straight, not too slack in your body, nor too tight. Relax your mind, not thinking of anything in the past or future. Rest in Natural Mind, but don't be too intense about it, thinking "I'm going to meditate now." Remember there is nothing to fix in the Natural State. Sustain that experience of being

in Natural Mind. If discursive thoughts arise, don't try to stop them, and don't follow after them. If you lose your awareness in the Natural State, bring it back.

3) Settle in the Natural State without effort or striving. Allow the awareness to remain as it is as thoughts arise and don't hold them tightly. Remain in the stillness. If you are distracted by thoughts that arise, come back to the stillness of the Natural State. Don't view any thoughts that arise in the mind as a problem. Remember the instructions of the teaching: to let them be is the base, viewing them as faulty is an error, allowing them to be released as they are is the method, not following after them is the path.

4) Since it is through meditation that we recognize this innate self-awareness, using these methods, try meditating now for a short while. Don't follow after thoughts; on the other hand, don't try to stop them either. If thoughts arise, just let them be; let them go and in that way you can recognize the Natural State. Whatever situations you have experienced in the past, forget them; just let them be. Don't occupy yourself with plans for the future. As

for the present moment of awareness, don't contrive anything; don't pollute it with anything, just rest in it. It is through not altering the present state of awareness and meditating within it, that you can recognize the innate self-knowing wisdom of the Natural State. The scriptures talk about a sky free of clouds. Just naturally remain in that state. If thoughts arise, don't think this is bad and try to stop them—that is not the method in this meditation. If we could speak of any effort, it is in viewing whatever thoughts or visions arise as like waves in the ocean. They arise from the ocean, they abide, and they settle back and dissolve into the ocean with the ocean being an example of the Natural State—all thoughts and visions dissolving back into it. If there is a very strong thought or vision that arises that you get involved with, shift away from developing concepts about it. Sometimes agitation may arise or your awareness may sink or you get drowsy. Just notice it, be aware that it happened, be alert. Sustain awareness as well as you can.

Questions and Answers

What is being taught here is actually something that is quite subtle and difficult to realize. It takes some time. In order to help people understand this very profound, subtle point, Buddha gave 84,000 teachings. Those teachings are meant to guide us closer and closer to this profound understanding, this profound meditation. Dzogchen presents this profound, subtle point in a very direct manner. Because this ultimate point is being revealed directly, there is no use for explanations of the five paths and ten stages—there is no discussion of that since the end result is being directly revealed. That basic nature, Natural Mind, from which all the various qualities and realizations arise, is what is being shown directly here. These instructions address how we go about manifesting it.

Q. You mentioned the practice called thögel, what is that? What is that technique?

A. There are two types of practices, *trechöd* (cutting

through) and *thögel* (direct crossing). It is said that thögel is for the really industrious practitioner. The reason for this is that thögel practice requires a lot of effort in order to get the subtle visions to arise. There are a lot of steps in thögel and eventually a time when those visions no longer arise. That's because with its attainment, the practitioner attains the rainbow body. They realize that their body is just a manifestation of the Natural State; their body actually becomes smaller and smaller and then disappears. When you reach high levels of thögel, the subtle visions of lights, rays and sounds disappear and the body disappears. Shardza Rinpoche was one who manifested this realization in 1935. His body shrunk down to the size of a cubit, the length of a forearm. His student, Dawa Dragpa, completely disappeared attaining rainbow body. Many lamas have manifested this realization. There were twenty-four masters from the beginning of the lineage of this oral transmission of Zhang Zhung Bön who realized rainbow body. The attainment comes primarily through thögel.

Q. *Is this a personal goal? It must take a long time.*

A. Yes. It does not always take a long time. Various practitioners' meditation can be different. It could be that entering into this practice, you develop the realization quickly. It definitely does not have to take years of poring over scriptures.

Q. Is there a cause for the arising, abiding and dissolving into the Natural State?

A. It's a matter of deception which involves the dualistic perception of a subject and object. Things that appear to us now are conventional phenomena which, in Tibetan, *kun zop (kun rdzob),* means completely obscured; we don't see them clearly. When we say they are obscured it means we see a false appearance; they are not true, they are illusions. We can make use of conventional phenomena in the world—a text, for instance—but when we analyze them in subtler ways we find that their nature is illusory.

Q. In the ultimate sphere, are there ultimate qualities?

A. We speak about its entity, nature, and compassion, its primordial purity and spontaneous accomplishment.

All the qualities of enlightened beings are spontaneously present within the Natural State. That is why studying and meditating on scriptures and deities has the power to bring improvement to our mind—because these aspects and qualities are present in the Natural State. In the Natural State these things spontaneously arise; there is no need for effort.

Q. *When you think about the endless number of forms and appearances within the Natural State, it's almost too big, it dissolves into it; it's infinite.*

A. I'm not talking about anything ending. There are the three unceasing bodies in the Natural State: Dharmakaya, and the form bodies, Sambhogakaya and Nirmanakaya. They are unceasing; this is important. There is no cessation, no ending in the Natural State, no true birth or exhaustion. When things dissolve into the Natural State you don't have to worry that they will be finished. The essential point is, when visions or thoughts arise in meditation, you don't try to stop them—because there is no cessation.

Q. *Sometimes people criticize Dzogchen and say it is incorrect. Why is that?*

A. It is a case of hearing these teachings, being frightened by them and misunderstanding them. When the Natural State is presented, there is a discussion of its being free from conceptuality. They misunderstand this and think that it is simply a method to stop thought. If that is all you're trying to do, it can dull your mind, cause rebirth as an animal, and so forth. But this is a misunderstanding of the balance; a correct understanding of both emptiness and clarity being involved. It is not just a matter of stopping thought. Thoughts continue to arise. In the middle turning of the wheel, the Perfection of Wisdom teachings, we hear pronouncements by Buddha that there is no form, no feeling, no perception and so on; all proclamations of the absence of things. This reveals a lack of production in phenomena; they are unborn, empty. Whereas, in the clarity of the Natural State there is a possibility for everything to arise and not cease. Negativity can be brought to cessation, but there is no cessation of existence or appearances. They are allowed to arise. This is not a nihilistic view. Thoughts are allowed to arise. When you go into a dark retreat and get visions of light, rays, and sounds, this is when you can gain real conviction that appearances do arise from the Natural State. It's not the eyes that are seeing, it's the mind itself; objects can be seen and letters can be read and written. This comes from a correct understanding of the awareness quality of the Natural State. There is a lineage of masters who have done this practice who have written about the experiences they've had.

Q. In this meditation of the Natural State, is there a way to use it as an object to develop shamatha?

A. If the Natural State is meditated upon correctly, it goes beyond the subject-object duality of shamatha meditation where there is a subjective mind focused on an object; it transcends that. But the practice of stabilizing the mind with shamatha meditation does provide a very good foundation or preparation for Dzogchen meditation.

Q. Does Dzogchen have the nine stages?

A. In the sutra and tantra traditions, it is explained that you have to pass through nine levels of mental placement in order to accomplish tranquil abiding. Those stages are not applied in Dzogchen teachings; you don't necessarily have to go through all nine levels. The first, second, third and fourth levels are sufficient. But if someone has perfected their shamatha meditation by passing through all nine levels, that's also excellent.

Q. *Is accomplishment of rainbow body full enlightenment or somewhere on the way to full enlightenment?*

A. It's pretty much a sign that, yes, someone has attained full enlightenment. Because all appearances are arising out of the Natural State. This is a sign that its nature is enlightenment. When all appearances are arising out of and dissolving back into Dharmakaya, that is, by definition, enlightenment.

Acknowledgements

I would like to extend my deepest gratitude for all those who translated, transcribed, reviewed, edited and contributed to these efforts in the production of this book: Prof. Kurt Keutzer who permitted me to use his translation of the root text, Jean and Bor Wen Huang, Donald Davies, David Molk, Kim Argula, Nancy Kvam, Antoniette Bauer and Kate Hitt.

—Geshe Dangsong Namgyal

Geshe Dangsong Namgyal

Geshe Dangsong Namgyal is a teacher, author, poet, and meditation master.

As a boy, he accompanied his father, ritual master of the Karshod in the Kham region of Tibet and undertook preliminary training. In 1985, he entered Lung Kar Monastery; then, under the advice of his teachers, he traveled to Menri Monastery, Sera Je Monastery and Triten Norbutse Monastery, where he studied with many of today's great masters. In 2013, after 25 years of training, he attained his Geshe degree.

He arrived in San Jose, California in 2013 and was the resident teacher at the Ananda Dharma Center.

Kunsang Gar Center was established in California as a religious nonprofit in 2016 and has since founded Kunsang Gar branches in Mexico and South America as well. As the founding spiritual director, Geshe continues to share Dharma teachings every week as part of his Kunsang Gar Wisdom Program in person and online.

He has written over twenty books in Tibetan and English on religion, culture, history and poetry. He is renowned for his knowledge of ancient script. His most recent Tibetan books have been volume one of a biography of the great master Chöden Rinpoche and an extensive accounting of the Guru Chowang Nyingma lineage, which was praised by H.H. Dalai Lama, H.H. 17th Karmapa, 12th H.E. Tai Situpa, and other great lamas. "Pure Dzogchen" and "Holy Women of Great Perfection" are his recent English publications. He has presented articles at many conferences throughout the world: Oxford University in England, Kobe University in Japan, France, India, Nepal, also the Science and Nonduality Conference in San Jose California.

He teaches Yungdrung bön and other Buddhist traditions and is a qualified Rimé *(Non-sectarian)* teacher. His aim is to share this ancient wisdom, serving all, without discrimination, beyond borders.

www.ingramcontent.com/pod-product-compliance
Lightning Source LLC
Chambersburg PA
CBHW070600010526
44118CB00012B/1392